Also by the Author

Representative Bureaucracy:
African American Mayors and Municipal Employment

So, You Think You Can Teach:
A Guide for the New College Professor in Teaching Adult Learners

Diversity Managers:
Angels of Mercy or Barbarians at the Gate

Crisis as a Platform for Social Change
from Strawberry Mansion to Silicon Valley

Thankful

Stephne

DR. SHELTON GOODE

WINTER IN AMERICA

THE IMPACT OF THE 2016 PRESIDENTIAL ELECTION ON
DIVERSITY IN COMPANIES, COMMUNITIES AND THE COUNTRY

outskirts
press

Outskirts Press, Inc.
http://www.outskirtspress.com

Paperback ISBN: 978-1-9772-0359-5
Hardback ISBN: 978-1-9772-0360-1

To

JR and Marcus, my sons, and

Kamden Alexander, my grandson, for their lives in a better world — I wish I had the ability to, and could I reach the nation's ear, I would, today, pour out a fiery stream of biting ridicule, blasting reproach, withering sarcasm and stern rebuke.

Contents

FOREWORD

It is not heat that is needed, but fire;
it is not the gentle shower, but a storm.

On election night, as it became clear that Donald Trump would be the country's next president, I found myself like a lot of people: feeling unsettled. As I watched the results trickle in and battleground states like Pennsylvania, Florida and North Carolina turned red on the TV map, I thought about my work as a diversity professional. I thought maybe — just maybe — this would be good for business. I also thought, maybe, it was time for a career change.

It's my job to help companies and communities create inclusive environments for people. For diversity professionals like myself, the election's polarizing nature, which especially divided the nation on issues of race, is twofold. While it meant some of my work would almost certainly boom, it also meant that a new set of challenges would emerge for me and other diversity professionals. It meant we would have to work harder to tamp down heightened feelings of fear and anxiety. We would have to be especially attentive as we listened to the concerns of people usually thought of as privileged. And we would have to be better at helping people navigate a language mine-field where the wrong word could ignite conflict.

Studying the maps of how people voted, I was disturbed by the stretch of red in my home town of Atlanta, a metropolis that is often celebrated for its diversity. Like many others in the field of diversity and inclusion, I equated a vote for Trump with a vote for intolerance. I believed that all my life's work had blown up in front of me. I have worked in the field of diversity and inclusion for more almost two decades and have managed diversity strategies for several Fortune

500 companies. On the one hand, I felt absolutely overwhelmed with the depth of how much work that had to be done. And on the other hand, I felt like I didn't even want to do the work. Given the results and how the map looked, I felt my work would be in vain.

It might feel futile, but many of my friends and colleagues who work in the field as diversity and inclusion consultants said they expected to see an increase in their business for the next four years. This made sense to me since the corporate world is a microcosm of the larger world. People who voted for Trump work at the same companies as those who voted for Hillary Clinton or other candidates. And in a contentious postelection environment, I predicted that employees would inevitably clash over matters of race, class, gender, sexual orientation, religion and political affiliation. I believed employees would file complaints with human resources, workplace ethics and compliance. As a result, diversity professionals like myself would be notified, and we would have to help managers in our respective organizations figure out how to deal with it all. For example, we would need to develop a whole new tool kit of language to help managers talk about this divisiveness and polarization. It's those who voted for Trump or support Trump and everyone else, and that's a difficult dichotomy to address, especially in the workplace.

One of the biggest tasks for diversity professionals is to break down any feelings that people are on opposing sides. The workplace is very tricky because what do you say if you want to remain friends with people? Some would suggest that you simply don't talk about politics and religion. And yet people are needing to talk about it. So, we need some ways to bring civility with caution and for people to feel that instead of doing an "us versus them," a "right versus wrong," it's "help me understand why you believe what you believe."

That "us versus them" sentiment is particularly tough to manage because of the 2016 presidential election. My work often involves helping people of color deal with historical garbage — like racism — while also helping white people who, I learned during the election campaign, feel strongly that they have never benefited from "white privilege." I think right now there's a temperament in the country of exclusion on both sides of the table, and those who have not been seen to have been historically excluded are feeling just as excluded as everyone else. It's seems we're in an era today where everyone is fighting in some ways over who's most excluded. Historically, it has been about women, people of color, people who are gay and lesbian. But today, white males feel they haven't been given their fair shake, and they want their viewpoint to be heard and accepted.

White people as a group, and particularly white men, don't typically make that list. But the 2016 presidential campaign unearthed a strong sentiment among white men who don't feel that they are a member of a group that has benefited from racial privilege, and if you look at their individual lives, some of them may not have benefited from privilege. Those of us in the field of diversity and inclusion have a responsibility to address everyone's concerns. It's not about a special effort toward white men. It's more than that — if you honor everybody's differences, they're more likely to own their privileges.

I believe this underscores the tension that diversity professionals, like the rest of the country, are tasked with resolving. Longstanding racial discord fueled by historical garbage collides with the idea of honoring everybody's differences when some of those differences spring from racial ignorance and racism. Thinking of all differences as equal is a problem. I think the backlash we're seeing is people who work in the diversity space — and social justice folks in general — are saying, "We are not going to be inclusive of ideas and values that are explicitly detrimental and harmful."

As a country, we have mastered the art of demonizing those we disagree with. The segmentation of the news and the hundreds of sources inundate us with information, yet we are less informed. We listen to those reporting their version of the news that we agree with. We talk past and through each other we don't agree with and demonization becomes the likely byproduct. I have engaged in it, so likely have you. It is time to stop this!

Even the phrase "diversity professional" can be divisive to some. Several of my colleagues are branding their work as "workplace inclusion" or "employee engagement" because many folks seem unable to admit that companies, communities, and yes, the country has a problem with the reality of diversity. My colleagues have responded by developing a workaround that is based on the concept that everyone is caught in a power differential in their respective companies. As a result, most of my colleagues are conducting training that has a lot to do with workplace inclusion and how it disproportionately affects those from different backgrounds.

My personal experience is that when I am conducting training, the minute I use words like "diversity," I lose half the room. Participants who equate diversity with people who are too "politically correct" will disengage and stop participating in the class. Most of the training I facilitate is about who you are as a person, and I don't focus on where you're from. You may be from middle America. You may root for the Jacksonville Jaguars. You might love barbecue. I'm a black man North Philadelphia. I grew up eating cheesesteaks and hoagies. I grew up in the ghetto. In the training I conduct, it's not about whether I'm politically correct or not. It's about how people feel different. I try to peel back the layers of the labels and help people connect.

All by himself, Donald Trump has normalized hate speech, overt bigotry and grossly disrespectful exchanges (both verbal and physical) between people. I had hoped at the end of the train wreck that was his presidential campaign, he would just go quietly into the night. What I learned on November 8, 2016, is that he not only won't go away, but he now will be front and center until November 8, 2020! And this helped me realize that the work moving forward is my and others' work, not Donald Trump's. It is about what you and I do moving forward in our sphere of control and influence. So, the work now shifts to how you and I respond to creating potential partnerships.

Donald Trump's ascendance to the oval office should provide a wake-up call to white men (and men in general) around the routinized minimization, objectification and vilification of women and should help them especially notice how powerful and confident women in leadership are often vilified. It is blatant sexism pure and simple. Donald Trump is right — the system is "rigged." The system is rigged against women, LGBTQ folk and people of color and will continue to be rigged until justice for all is a reality for all.

In this book, I will share my take on some of the lessons learned and the way forward. While much will be fought in Congress, in the courts, and on the streets, my focus, after some reflection on what happened and why, will be on implications for the corporate arena. Also, a note to those who have followed my writing: while my political leanings are no secret, I have had a philosophy in my writing and tweeting to not take on a partisan tone that seeks to diminish or refute the stances and choices of those with different political views. Instead, I have continually focused, in a more observant and interpretative way, on the cultural implications of sociopolitical and economic forces and sought to contribute to a contemporary vision of society that embraces greater diversity through inclusion. In this journey, I have been able to successfully engage with people across the political spectrum.

But in this moment, I need to make a specific pivot. The 2016 election has moved the discourse and behavioral implications way outside the margins of what had been political debate even as the quality and appropriateness of that debate has deteriorated since November 8, 2016. But even with this degradation, I still felt it important to honor and respect the vast range of different political views of people I disagree with.

But the explicitness of Trump administration's racism, homophobia, xenophobia, Islamophobia and misogyny are a declaration that he wants to stand outside that arena of decency and mutual respect. So, I pivot to explicit condemnation of Donald Trump's behavior and will write accordingly.

I also make a key distinction between Donald Trump's behavior and that of Trump's supporters. While there is a disturbingly high percentage of those Trump supporters who are full-throated in their advocacy of Trump's policies and behaviors, there is also a high percentage of those who aren't. And these are the ones we must find a way to reengage with if we have any hope of maximizing the diversity and enhancing inclusion in our companies, communities and the country.

In the first chapter of the book, I discuss that there is one undeniable fact: one side lost, and one side won, but everybody needs to get together, so we can all move forward. Walking that line of competing interests is made even tougher by the language of diversity, including the word "diversity" itself. I talked to several of my colleagues, and they revealed that they are actively avoiding language that might be polarizing so they can keep everyone in the conversation. They concede that in the 2016 presidential election, nearly 45 million people voted, and they assume that half of the participants they are working with daily voted for Trump, half for Clinton. So, figuring out what tone to strike is important.

In chapter 2, I argue that it is entirely possible — and many agree — that Hillary Clinton would be the president of the United States if the former FBI director, James Comey, had not sent a letter to Congress about her emails in the last weeks of the campaign. But the electoral trends that put Donald J. Trump within striking distance of victory were clear long before Mr. Comey sent his letter. They were clear before WikiLeaks published hacked emails from the Democratic National Committee. They were even clear in early July 2016, before Mr. Comey excoriated Hillary Clinton for using a private email server.

Chapter 3 addresses the questions: How does the country move on after one of the most bitter, nasty and divisive presidential campaigns in history? How do we become one nation? Invoking the legacy of Abraham Lincoln, Donald Trump promised to heal America's divisions even as he threatened to sue his female accusers and insinuated that the election was rigged. Trump might be ill-suited to serve as "healer in chief," but that does not mean that the country cannot heal itself. Other countries damaged by conflict have tackled the issue of reconciliation and come up with an effective formula.

In chapter 4, I explain how political analysts have talked about how ignorance, racism, sexism, nationalism, Islamophobia, economic disenfranchisement and the decline of the middle class contributed to the popularity of Donald Trump in rural America. But this misses the deeper cultural factors that shape the thinking of the conservatives who live and work in the "red" states where Trump won the popular vote.

Chapter 5 examines how after the 2016 presidential election, the country entered into uncharted times with the rising neoconservative, white nationalist and racist influence on American society. These forces are seeking to reverse and disturb cultures of inclusion and respectability for all citizens. However, diversity and inclusion are part of the American fabric of life that must not change due to the 2016 presidential election or other political changes. If one studies history, we can see similar disruptions. The question for the diversity and inclusion professional is "how do we remain relevant during these times and continue our momentum toward a more inclusive society in general and a more respectful climate in our workplaces?"

Chapter 6 describes how US cities are rapidly becoming more diverse, but that doesn't mean they are more inclusive. In fact, in many large metro areas, some minority groups are now more segregated from white populations than before, according to an analysis of new US census data by the Brookings Institution. Minorities are driving population growth in large metropolitan areas — they've accounted for 98 percent of it since 2000, per Brookings demographer William Frey, who crunched five-year estimates from the American Community Survey. That is quickly shifting the racial and ethnic makeup of US cities.

In chapter 7, I discuss how thousands of people have struggled with how to put the pieces back together and move forward as one country with many voices, faces and legacies. Some may dismiss the figures of speech used by candidates in the 2016 presidential election as common "political tropes." But others see incredibly tainted and damaging language in speeches and debates, filled with both coded and blatant references to race, stereotypes of communities of color, immigrant scapegoating and divisive suggestions of isolation, barriers and "otherness."

In chapter 8, I discuss the fact that the presidential campaign was incredibly divisive along the lines of gender, education and ethnicity. The spike in the number of hate crimes immediately following the election demonstrates how deep the fractures go in our society, and how exclusion — from economic opportunity or by a hyper-focus on diversity — is being deeply felt and experienced by so many. The inevitable, and uncomfortable, conclusion is that many of us were not aware of, or didn't prioritize, full inclusion — in our lives, in our organizations and in our society. Given this collective blind spot, and the reality of the Trump Administration , what will companies, communities and the country do differently if we truly believe in the transformative power of valuing differences? The need for inclusiveness is greater than ever.

Can the workplace serve as a healing space? I explore this question in chapter 9 and discuss that CEOs know that inside their corporate, store, plant and factory walls flow the full crosscurrents of a polarized employees stoked by poisonous rhetoric. But they are unsure of how best to lead in these dangerous times. Do they just hope that employees will keep their thoughts and feelings to themselves while they are at work? They quickly recognize this "head in the sand" approach will not be sustainable nor helpful.

I discuss in chapter 10 that because of the 2016 presidential election results, we are witnessing an impassioned debate playing out in our political and cultural worlds. Should we serve our own interests or the broader interests? Should we put America first or our own community? Should we place our company's interests first, our customers' interests or the environment? Should we place our career success as primary or our team's success? The answer to these and other salient questions is obvious. "Yes." We need to do it all.

ACKNOWLEDGMENTS

From the length of these acknowledgments, it may read more like an Academy Award acceptance speech than a simple thank-you. I know my editor is rolling her eyes because she is always counseling me to be brief. But it is important that I thank the many people who helped me bring this vision to reality. Whether it was emotional support, interviews, editorial help, research or supplying the thousands of pieces of information that make a book like this possible, I could not have accomplished it without the people listed here.

While the responsibility for the final product is clearly my own, I am indebted to numerous scholars and diversity and inclusion professionals for their helpful comments and critical suggestions on various aspects of the book. The journey to this final product has been informed mainly by my professional experiences and personal perspectives presented here, along with input from several of the top thought leaders on managing diversity in companies and communities.

There would be no book, of course, if not for the family, friends and professional colleagues who were generous and brave enough to share with me their personal views on diversity in America. This kind of candor and courage is a lot to ask for and even harder to repay. The practical insights helped me write several chapters. In no order, these include the following contributors: Jim Rogers, Jennifer Brown, Steve Paskoff and Bill Proudman. Special thanks go out to my wife, Pamela Goode, who inspired me to write this book and offered important insights and encouragement.

I presented an earlier version of the book to some of my former students from Troy University, Georgia State, and Duke University. Their critique and feedback helped shape several of my conclusions.

As an adjunct professor at several colleges and universities, I have the privilege of interacting with some of the brightest and most energetic students I have encountered in my 20 years of teaching. They forced me to rethink several ideas, and they constantly challenged my basic assumptions about the concept of diversity in America.

I am especially indebted to my friends and colleagues I have had the privilege of working and laughing with. Over the years, my family, friends and colleagues have helped me hone my ideas and improve my writing and teaching on diversity and inclusion. As a result, I have been able to contribute more fully to the development of a new generation of diversity and inclusion leaders.

Every author needs practical help in addition to inspiration and encouragement. I am blessed to have had so many publishing professionals who dedicated many hours to this project. Kristin Thiel deserves special mention for her meticulous editing of the manuscript and critical feedback throughout the preparation of the final draft. The final stages of permissions, copyediting and meeting the publisher's deadlines would have been impossible without her help. I also thank her for critical comments on sections of this book and on related research work.

A special shout-out goes to Elaine Simpson, who was my critical liaison with the publisher during the hectic process of finalizing the book for publication. She provided me much-needed guidance and professional expertise. I was thrilled to work with Elaine, who called on her considerable humor, warmth and expertise to guide me through the often stressful and confusing process of publishing my third book. Special appreciation goes to Pat Wilson, another member of the Outskirts Press, whose expert and sensitive advice clearly enhanced both the readability and value of the book.

Finally, I would like to thank my family, who are my pride and my joy, and to whom this book is dedicated. I love you all.

Chapter 1 —
First Minute of a New Day

We need a storm, a whirlwind and an earthquake.

Introduction

By now, everyone has their 2016 presidential election "day af-ter" story. Mine started with a 3:00 a.m. text on November 9, 2016, from my friend, saying, "How could this happen?" I texted back, "Please call me." I was awake anyway, having been up for hours and unable to get to sleep. I happened to be in Wisconsin on a busi-ness trip and had watched the election results come in with several of my colleagues. We started the evening at a local pizza place with a TV hung in the corner, next to which was a framed picture of the 1968 Green Bay Packers — a symbol reminding all of us that we were far from home. The five of us sat at the table, gripping each other while we watched the map go red and the opportunity to elect a female president go dark. Three of us were white and from Chi-cago, one was Hispanic and from Baltimore and one was black and from Atlanta. All five of us were in disbelief, wondering what planet we lived on.

As the evening wore on, and the reality of the situation hit, all I could think about was how I was going to explain this to my sons. I was already upset that I couldn't be with them in Texas as they watched the results come in, and we exchanged a few calls and texts earlier in the evening. At 6:30 a.m., I was still up and watching the news coverage, knowing that was not going to change anything. When my friend finally called me at 6:30 a.m., I could hear the stress and anger in her voice. We both had been extremely plugged in to the campaigns and election in our own unique ways.

I watched all three debates and watched all the subsequent *Saturday Night Live* parodies, laughing and believing that there no way that Donald Trump would win the election. All I could think about, alone in my Wisconsin hotel room in my dazed state, was how the country would get through the next four years.

Feeling totally powerless and drained, I decided to write my sons, both active-duty members of the US Armed Forces, an email. I needed them to have answers to "How?" and "Why?" Here is an excerpt:

"The news is not what we expected. I know we are all stunned. I have many friends and colleagues who are wondering how to explain this unexpected and undesired outcome. I do not have a good explanation for you...But I do know this. The love and pride I have for you knows no bounds. You have a new commander in chief, but your job is the same. We're counting on you to keep us safe and to continue to do everything within your power to make sure that no weapon formed against us ever prospers. I also know that we will get through this. We are family, and we can endure the toughest obstacles. We are African Americans, and we are survivors. You have African heritage and will fight for what we believe is right. No matter what happens, I want you to know that I believe in you, and we will support you...I cannot wait to see you again and hug you and hold you and remind you that we are a family, and nothing can break that."

The presidential election results of 2016 made me wanna holler and throw up both my hands! Not so much because my candidate lost but because the ascendance of Trump to the presidency was so shocking and saddening to me due to his questionable character and abhorrent behavior. For months prior to the election, I watched him

2

routinely and publicly denigrate women, immigrants, Muslims, black and brown folks and the disabled, among others. He, with the help of the major press and ultra-right social media outlets, normalized this bullying behavior. This, in turn, had a ripple effect, lowering the bar for others to propagate hurtful and hateful language and behavior. Immediately after the election there was an increasing number of incidents of hate speech, verbal intimidation and physical confrontation. Following the election many took the streets in protest as thousands expressed feeling more fearful and unsure.

Donald Trump's repeated behavior toward women showed a gross disrespect, objectification, misogyny and sexism such that if any other man displayed similar behavior in any professional setting it would result in their dismissal. Yet now he is the president. For me, his election to the presidency is a personal call to action. I will not just sit on the sidelines and despair.

Standing back from my initial shock and sadness on postelection night, I realized this. This is not about Trump. This is about how we respond to and show up with each other. The election has acted as a catalyst, and as time has gone by, the election has given me more clarity about my work going forward.

We as a country are more divided and polarized than ever. We find temporary solidarity and pseudo-comfort with those most like us. We routinely vilify and demonize others most different than ourselves. "Our truth" gets confused with "THE TRUTH." We think we are more informed, but really, we are only looking at our own version of reality with others who agree with us. We talk past, over or through others.

My thinking got a powerful boost from a Facebook post from an old friend, Bill Proudman, whom I met years earlier when I worked at Georgia Power. Bill's words helped snap me back to a new and heightened sense of reality about my own work moving forward.

3

"We will be fine; we will take it all in and figure out what happened, what it all means and most importantly what we must do to work together to get it right for everyone. The world isn't going to explode; in fact, I believe it serves as a huge wake-up call, and we must all respond intelligently to keep our collective worst fears from manifesting themselves. So, spend a minute in shock, or anger, but only a minute, because when you're done with that, the challenges we've faced for decades will still be there. Unless you pray and use the intelligence that God gave you to navigate this new political system and all the appointments, including Supreme Court appointments, Cabinet, etc., you may consume yourself with what Trump has said during the campaign, what HRC did or did not do, trust issues, charisma issues and a host of other things that don't matter at this point. Let's work together for common good my friends."

Bill's words, "we will be fine," helped me to realize that for me and many other people of color and women, Donald Trump's words are simply lifting the curtain for Bill and other white men on the almost daily inequities, slights and egregious actions many women and people of color face in this country. One of the things I realized now from all this is how many white men are realizing what people of color and white women have been saying and navigating for decades.

After the election, I realized that I and others who were disappointed in election results face a series of choice points. The choice points mostly revolve around how we choose to come to partnership with others across the divide of perceived difference. Going forward, we diversity professionals would be faced with choices about how to respond.

I challenge my colleagues in the field of diversity and inclusion to ask the question: in the wake of the 2016 presidential election, what is my personal work to be the change I wish to see where everyone feels valued, heard and respected? With all this, I find myself with a growing sense of energy for the work ahead. I find myself saying, "Deal me in," and I want to ask all of us, especially diversity professionals, "Are you in as well?"

I am determined to lean in, using inclusion and engagement as the tools of choice to partner across the void of intolerance and bigotry, both in my community and across the country. Now is the time to lean toward rather than away from each other. So, you say, "Shelton, what should I do?" My answer is that I believe there are several small but significant acts of courage each of us can take to strengthen the bridge of inclusion in our companies, communities and the country:

- Engage with others. Reach out and speak your truth while being respectful of others. Invite others to speak their truth as well.
- Know that your way or approach is just that, YOUR WAY. It is no more right or wrong than someone else's. It just is. Notice and feel what you and others feel. Bridging difference with others is an emotional — not just an intellectual — process.
- Listen deeply to understand another's perspective (especially when you disagree). Don't confuse understanding with agreement.
- Work from within your own sphere of influence and then expand it.
- Choose love in the form of patience, empathy and courage. Do not succumb to hate. Know and use your support systems. Seek them out, so you don't feel isolated and alone.

- Figure out your own personal work. Understand and probe your self-interest to support and stand in solidarity with other historically marginalized people.
- Pay attention to the gap between intention and impact — in both your interactions with others and theirs with you. Work always to close it.

Together we can bridge and close the divide that was magnified by the 2016 presidential election. Together we can prevent it from tearing us apart — neighbor to neighbor, work colleague to work colleague and even family member to family member. Whatever President Trump does or doesn't do, speak out and advocate for the change that is essential to all in our world. I will be the change I wish to see, and so should you. Join with me and other courageous change agents. Figure out how to hang in there with others over the long haul. Together we can and must be the change to find our critical common ground and common good.

As I look ahead, I believe that now, more than ever, diversity professionals like me must take a harder look at our practices, both in terms of how we will frame training and how we will choose clients. It's not enough to be able to empathize with different groups who are feeling attacked. We must be an ally, which means we must defend and speak up. When you're at lunch or dinner or on a break and someone makes a disparaging joke about anyone, let's say Muslims or Jews or being gay, don't let it pass! I encourage you to pause that statement, and maybe you simply say, "That's unacceptable, and I don't appreciate that language!"

Since the 2016 presidential election, I have spent a lot of time thinking about the best way those of us in the diversity profession can be more effective and take our work to a new level. I think we should all begin by agreeing not to consult with companies or communities that normalize intolerance or discrimination or attempt to brush them under the rug. Let's hold community and company leaders accountable for demonstrating a sincere and real commitment to diversity. For example, there are number of CEOs who have doubled down on their diversity efforts since the election. The top leaders of AT&T, Starbucks, PepsiCo, General Electric, Apple, Medtronic and others have shown demonstrable support for diversity and inclusion both inside their respective companies and their communities. For example, Medtronic CEO Omar Ishrak, in an email to the medical device-maker's employees, took a stand that would surely be heartening to those who do the work of diversity. He called the company's principles around inclusion "an irrevocable priority." Another example of courageous leadership was shown by Randall Stephenson, the CEO of AT&T. He spoke to employees at the company's National Employee Resource Groups conference in Dallas, Texas, and challenged employees to seek understanding about the causes of the country's racial tensions and to engage in crucial conversations. He ended by saying that he wasn't asking the group to be merely "tolerant" of each other. "Tolerance is for cowards," he said. "Being tolerant requires nothing from you but to be quiet and to not make waves, holding tightly to your views and judgments without being challenged. Do not tolerate each other. Work hard, move into uncomfortable territory and understand each other. If this is a dialogue that's going to begin at AT&T, I feel like it probably ought to start with me."

Call to Action for the Diversity Profession

CNBC, CNN and other news media seem to be reacting to the various tweets that Trump is pushing out, which have affected some

7

company stock values. Even the *Washington Post* has reported that business leaders are feeling unnerved by the leadership style of president. While this topsy-turvy approach is affecting business stocks, as diversity practitioners, we need to help our senior leaders remain calm and focused on the long-term talent needs of our companies.

Over the years, I have learned that knee-jerk reactions to decision-making with regards to diversity and inclusion are not effective in the long run, especially when there are still too many unknowns. Following are some things we do need to think about as diversity practitioners as we continue to deal with the fallout from the 2016 presidential election.

- **Employee Law and Regulation:** The Trump administration, like previous Republican-led administrations, has traditionally focused less legislation on social justice and more on pro-business employment strategies. We can already see this unfolding with the Overtime Work Rule being challenged and slowed down. Chances are we will see an easing up of EEOC/OFFCP investigations and more relaxed guidelines. However, a lot of this will depend on the Department of Labor; however, if history repeats itself, we will see less focus on labor and compliance. There are two areas that we know for sure the Trump administration will continue to focus on: immigration and the increase in the hourly wage rate.
- **Immigration Legislation:** Laws related to H1B Visa compliance will continue to be a focus area for the Trump administration, as well as exportation of jobs. There has been consistent conversations and comments prior to the 2016 presidential election, and currently there appears to be a continued focus in these areas. The companies that will most likely be impacted are those that have relied on immigrant

workforces for highly skilled technology and science work-ers and/or those that are dependent on temporary immigrant labor for field and manual jobs. As a result, we may see more automation in field labor employment.

- **Health Care:** The Affordable Care Act and other health care issues will continue to be a target of the Trump administra-tion. We can expect that regardless of what is done, there will be a lot of back and forth in the House of Representa-tives and Senate on this topic. In addition, whatever the agreement turns out to be there, will be at least a two-three-year lag in implementation. The US health care challenge is much like the Brexit vote — not until you start to look at the details will people realize that verbalizing an exit is much easier than the actual untangling of the system.

- **Talent Management:** A major challenge for companies will continue to be talent attraction and retention. Regardless of the type of company or business, a well-thought-out plan to attract and retain talent will be critical regardless of the de-cisions and legislation the Trump administration comes up with. So, investment in tools and resources that allow com-panies to focus on analyzing workforce demographics and managing knowledge transfer while keeping labor costs in check will continue to be critical. We are entering the era of workforce analytics, and any company that does not get its arms around this will struggle.

- **Diversity and Inclusion Disruption:** While there are a few major companies committed to diversity and inclusion — as evidenced by the decreasing number of stand-alone diversity departments — there is a need for greater alignment of di-versity and inclusion with the overall business strategy. This does not mean that companies will deemphasize past work,

9

but hiring diverse candidates especially in the technical and sciences areas will become more competitive. This is simply because as a country we don't have enough people graduating in these fields. There have been several studies that show companies with women in senior leadership roles have better ROI. In addition, companies with high turnover rates have a higher talent replacement cost than those with low turnover. Some areas where diversity and inclusion can help play a key role is in driving innovation and developing creative business solutions or developing new products to market as well as building the company's brand by connecting with consumers. The biggest challenge for diversity practitioners is how to show the ROI of programs.

- **Corporate Culture:** With an improved fiscal economy, one of the biggest challenges companies will be facing is retaining workers, so investing in programs designed to strengthen and improve corporate culture will become even more important. In tough economic times, employees tend to stay with companies longer, but in healthy and robust fiscal economies, diverse talent, particularly among Millennials and Gen Xers, tends to change jobs more quickly. The strongest talent of the organization tends to jump first. Companies that don't have strong core values and a corporate culture that is inclusive and flexible will still be financially viable but will have to work harder to retain talent especially in a stronger and more vibrant economy. While companies have continued to invest in employee engagement tools and programs, a 2016 Gallup study of eighty thousand employees nationally showed that a significant portion of the workforce remains disengaged, and so organizations that will thrive are those

10

that will be able to develop a strong corporate culture and retain diverse talent.

- **Workforce Development Programs:** Because of a lack of skilled labor, we will see greater investment on behalf of companies on apprenticeship programs offered through technical schools and community colleges to address the skill gaps in critical industries. In addition, we will see companies develop and implement retooling programs designed to help employees who might have exited stay with the company and gain new skill sets. In the past, federal dollars have been available to organizations from the Departments of Labor, Energy, Commerce and Transportation, which made it possible for companies to get funding for apprenticeship programs. However, it is now uncertain if future funding will be available from the federal government. Regardless of whether future federal funding is available for these kinds of programs, it makes sense to grow specific skills and retain talent. These programs have historically yielded positive business results and business savings for major companies in manufacturing and the energy sector.

Implications for Diversity in America

As diversity practitioners, we need to keep in mind we need to be adaptable to changes following the 2016 presidential election, and we need to help our respective companies develop a well-thought plan grounded in the company's workforce needs. This is critical to avoiding short-term reactions.

11

Chapter 2 — Separating Election Myths and Facts

The pulse of the country must be quickened;
the conscience of America must be awakened.

Introduction

It is entirely possible, as many have argued, that Hillary Clinton would be the president of the United States if the former FBI director, James Comey, had not sent a letter to Congress about her emails in the last weeks of the campaign. But the electoral trends that put Donald J. Trump within striking distance of victory were clear long before Mr. Comey sent his letter. They were clear before WikiLeaks published hacked emails from the Democratic National Committee. They were even clear back in July 2016, before Mr. Comey excoriated Hillary Clinton for using a private email server.

It was clear from the start that Hillary Clinton was struggling to tap into the diversity that fueled the Obama coalition. At every point of the race, Donald Trump was doing better among white voters without a college degree than Mitt Romney did in 2012 — by a wide margin. Hillary Clinton was also not matching Mr. Obama's support among black voters. This was the core of the Obama coalition: an alliance between black voters and Northern white voters, from Mr. Obama's first win in the 2008 Iowa caucuses to his final sprint across the so-called Midwestern firewall states where he staked his 2012 reelection bid.

The Obama Coalition Crumbled

The countryside of Iowa and the industrial belt along Lake Erie are not the sorts of places that people envision when they think of the Obama coalition. Yet they were important components of his victory. History shows that President Obama won thanks to a young, diverse, well-educated and metropolitan "coalition of the ascendant" — an emerging Democratic majority anchored in the new economy. Hispanic voters were credited with Mr. Obama's victory. But Mr. Obama would have won reelection even if he hadn't won the Hispanic vote at all. He would have won even if the electorate had been as old and as white as it had been in 2004.

Largely overlooked, his key support often came in the places where you would least expect it. He did better than John Kerry and Al Gore among white voters across the Northern United States, despite exit poll results to the contrary. Overall, 34 percent of Mr. Obama's voters were whites without a college degree — larger in number than black voters, Hispanic voters or well-educated whites.

In most Northern states, white voters shifted left. In the South, the opposite happened. He excelled in a nearly continuous swath from the Pacific Coast of Oregon and Washington to the Red River Valley in Minnesota, along the Great Lakes to the coast of Maine. In these places, Mr. Obama often ran as strong or stronger than any Democrat in history.

In 2016, Donald Trump made huge gains among white working-class voters. It wasn't just in the places where Democratic strength had been eroding for a long time, like western Pennsylvania. It was often in the places where Democrats had seemed resilient or even strong, like Scranton, Pennsylvania, and eastern Iowa.

It was a decisive break from previous election trends. White voters without college degrees for the first time deviated from the national trend and swung decidedly toward the Republicans. No bastion of white working-class Democratic strength was immune to the trend. For the first time in the history of the two parties, the Republican candidate did better among low-income whites than among affluent whites, according to exit poll data and a compilation of *New York Times/CBS News* surveys.

According to exit polls, Donald Trump did better than Mr. Romney by twenty-four points among white voters without a degree making less than $30,000 a year. He won these voters by a margin of 62 to 30 percent, compared with Mr. Romney's narrow win of 52 percent to 45 percent. In general, exit poll data should be interpreted with caution — but pre-election polls showed a similar swing, and the magnitude of the shifts most likely withstands any failings of the exit polls.

Hillary Clinton's profound weakness among Northern, white, working-class voters was not expected. She was thought to be strong among the older, white, working-class voters who were skeptical of Mr. Obama from the start. Most of Mr. Obama's strength among white voters without a degree was due to his gains among those under age forty-five. But Donald Trump expanded on Republican gains among older, working-class, white voters, while erasing most of Mr. Obama's gains among younger, Northern, white voters without a degree. His gains among younger, working-class whites were especially important in the Upper Midwest. Young, white, working-class voters represented a larger share of the vote there than anywhere else in the country. Mr. Obama's strength among them — and Hillary Clinton's weakness — was evident from the beginning of the 2008 primaries.

It Wasn't Turnout

Donald Trump's gains among white working-class voters weren't simply caused by Democrats staying home on Election Day.

The Clinton team knew what was wrong from the start. Clinton's election models, based on survey data, indicated that they were underperforming Mr. Obama in less-educated white areas by a wide margin — perhaps ten points or more — as early as May 2016.

The campaign looked back to respondents who were contacted in 2012 and found many white working-class voters who had backed Mr. Obama were now supporting Donald Trump. The same story was obvious in public polls of registered voters. Those polls were not affected by changes in turnout.

But the limited data that's already available is consistent with the story evident in the preselection polling: Turnout wasn't the major factor driving shifts among white voters. The voter-file data in North Carolina showed that the turnout among white Democrats and Republicans increased by almost the exact amount — about 2.5 percent. The same was true in Florida.

Nationally, there is no relationship between the decline in Democratic strength and the change in turnout. Donald Trump made gains in white working-class areas, whether turnout surged or dropped. The exit polls also showed all the signs that Donald Trump was winning over Obama voters. Perhaps most strikingly, Donald Trump won 19 percent of white voters without a degree who approved of Mr. Obama's performance, including 8 percent of those who "strongly" approved of Mr. Obama's performance and 10 percent of white working-class voters who wanted to continue Mr. Obama's policies. Donald Trump won 20 percent of self-identified liberal, white working-class voters, according to the exit polls, and 38 percent of those who wanted policies that were more liberal than Mr. Obama's. It strongly suggests that Donald Trump won over large numbers of white working-class voters who supported Mr. Obama four years earlier.

Trump Used Obama's Playbook

The notion that Donald Trump could win over so many people who voted for Mr. Obama and who still approved of his performance is hard to understand for people with ideologically consistent views on a traditional liberal-conservative spectrum. Donald Trump, if anything, was Mr. Obama's opposite. But the two had the same winning pitch to white working-class voters.

Mr. Obama and his campaign team portrayed Mr. Romney as a plutocrat who dismantled companies and outsourced jobs. The implication was that he would leave middle-class jobs prey to globalization and corporations.

The proof of Mr. Obama's commitment to the working class and Mr. Romney's callousness, according to the Obama campaign, was the auto bailout: Mr. Obama protected the auto industry; Mr. Romney wrote "Let Detroit Go Bankrupt" in the *New York Times*. There was one place where Mr. Romney could effectively argue that he could protect the industrial economy and the people who worked in it: coal country. There he made big gains after the Obama administration pushed climate-change policies that would reduce the production and use of coal.

In retrospect, the scale of the Democratic collapse in coal country was a harbinger of just how far the Democrats would fall in their old strongholds once they forfeited the mantle of working-class interests. Donald Trump owned Mr. Obama's winning message to autoworkers and Mr. Romney's message to coal country. He didn't merely run to protect the remnants of the industrial economy; he promised to restore it and "make America great again."

Just as Mr. Obama's team caricatured Mr. Romney, Donald Trump caricatured Hillary Clinton as a tool of Wall Street, bought by special interests. She, too, would leave workers vulnerable to the forces of globalization and big business, he said. According to Donald Trump's campaign, the proof of his commitment to the working class wasn't the auto bailout but the issue of trade: Donald Trump said free trade was responsible for deindustrialization and asserted that he would get tough on China, renegotiate NAFTA and pull out of the Trans-Pacific Partnership — two trade agreements that Hillary Clinton supported or helped negotiate (she later rejected the Trans-Pacific deal).

Like Mr. Obama, Donald Trump ran against the establishment — and against a candidate who embodied it far more than John McCain or Mr. Romney did. The various allegations against Hillary Clinton neatly complemented the notion that she wasn't out to help ordinary Americans.

Taken together, Donald Trump's views on immigration, trade, China, crime, guns and Islam all had considerable appeal to white working-class Democratic voters. It was a far more appealing message than old Republican messages about abortion, same-sex marriage and entitlement programs such as Medicare, Medicaid and Social Security.

The Impact of White Working-Class Democrats

Donald Trump's economic views appealed to blue-collar, white Democrats. None of this is to say that changes in turnout didn't help Donald Trump at all. It's just not the reason he made such large gains among white working-class voters. There was no relationship between the change in Democratic support and the change in turnout or the change in turnout and Democratic strength. But the Democrats did have a turnout problem in November 2016. It wasn't a broad Democratic turnout problem. It was a black turnout problem.

Fade to Black

The turnout probably increased among all major groups of voters — Hispanics, white Democrats, white Republicans — except black voters. The conclusive data is available in the Southern states where voters indicate their race on their voter registration forms, and they point toward a considerable decline in black turnout.

In Georgia, the black share of the electorate fell to 27.6 percent from 29.9 percent, and in Louisiana, it fell to 28.5 percent from 30.1 percent. In North Carolina, the black share of the electorate was below 21 percent of voters — down from 23 percent in 2012. In Florida, the black turnout fell by a similar amount — to 12.7 percent of voters from 14 percent. In these states, the black share of the electorate was higher than it was in 2004. It just wasn't as high as it was with Mr. Obama at the top of the ticket in 2008 and 2012.

Young black voters were a key driver of the decline. They registered at a lower rate than they did ahead of the 2012 and 2008 presidential elections, causing the black share of registered voters to dip. And those who were registered turned out at a far lower rate than black registrants did in 2012. Turnout dropped by 8 percent in the majority black wards of Philadelphia, while rising everywhere else in the city. The turnout in Detroit fell by 14 percent. Turnout fell in other industrial centers with a large black population, like Milwaukee, Wisconsin, and Flint, Michigan. It's hard to know just how much of this is lower black turnout instead of black population decline — the census can struggle to make population estimates in places with a declining population — but the turnout certainly dropped faster than the reported population decline.

Taken in totality, it appears that black turnout dropped somewhere between 5 percent and 10 percent — with few exceptions. It should be noted that the decline in black turnout appears very consistent across the country, regardless of whether states put in new laws designed to reduce turnout, like those cutting early voting or requiring a photo ID.

Was the decline in black turnout enough to change the result of the election? It seems so. If black turnout in 2016 had matched 2012 levels, Hillary Clinton would have almost certainly scratched out wins in Wisconsin, Michigan and Pennsylvania. Florida and North Carolina would have been extremely close. But pinning Hillary Clinton's loss on low black turnout would probably be a mistake. Mr. Obama would have easily won both his elections with this level of black turnout and support. He would have won Michigan, Ohio and Wisconsin each time even if Detroit, Cleveland and Milwaukee had been severed from their states and cast adrift into the Great Lakes. Perhaps more important, the Clinton campaign's models and public polls all assumed lower black turnout — and still showed Hillary Clinton on track for victory.

The Clinton Coalition Fell Short

The Clinton campaign believed it could compensate for the loss of the Obama coalition by winning the so-called rising American electorate or coalition of the ascendant of well-educated voters and Hispanic voters — a caricature of the Obama coalition. These demographic shifts have benefited Democrats over the last decade, but most of these gains have come in noncompetitive states. Demographic shifts helped turn Nevada and Virginia blue in the last decade but weren't enough to flip Texas, Georgia or Arizona.

For example, in 2016, the exit polls exaggerated the importance of well-educated and Hispanic voters. In 2012, these voters won the election for Mr. Obama — and in 2016, they lost it for Hillary Clinton. According to the election results, Hillary Clinton fared worse among white voters — but much worse among Hispanic, Asian American and black voters than Mr. Obama. And the election results show that she didn't win well-educated white voters, as many pre-selection polls predicted.

The analysis of voting returns, census and pre-election polling data suggests that Hillary Clinton was stronger among well-educated white and nonwhite voters than the exit polls imply. It is important to emphasize that these estimates are preliminary. They will change over the next few years with more data from the Census Bureau and additional polling. But it nonetheless paints an alternative picture that's more consistent with the actual results, the pre-election polls and the consensus of academics and campaign analysts on the electorate.

Well-Educated White Voters Weren't Enough

The analysis suggests that Hillary Clinton was the first Democrat to win white voters with a college degree. Election results show that Hillary Clinton did better among well-educated white and Hispanic voters than was reflected in the exit polls. Hillary Clinton's gains were concentrated among the most affluent and best-educated white voters, much as Donald Trump's gains were concentrated among the lowest-income and least-educated white voters.

Hillary Clinton gained seventeen points among white postgraduates, according to several estimates, but just four points among whites with a bachelor's degree. There was a similar pattern by income. Over all, she picked up twenty-four points among white voters with a degree making more than $250,000, according to the exit polls, while she made only slight gains among those making less than $100,000 per year. These gains helped her win huge margins in the most well-educated and prosperous liberal bastions of the new economy, like Manhattan, Silicon Valley, Washington, DC, Seattle, Chicago and Boston. There, Hillary Clinton ran up huge margins in traditionally liberal enclaves and stamped out nearly every wealthy precinct that supported the Republicans.

Scarsdale, New York, voted for Hillary Clinton by fifty-seven points, up from Mr. Obama's eighteen-point win. You could drive a full thirty miles through the leafy suburbs northwest of Boston before reaching a town where Donald Trump hit 20 percent of the vote. She won the affluent eastside suburbs of Seattle, like Mercer Island, Bellevue and Issaquah, by around fifty points — doubling Mr. Obama's victory.

Every old-money Republican enclave of western Connecticut, like Darien and Greenwich, voted for Hillary Clinton, in some cases swinging thirty points in her direction. Every precinct of Winnetka and Glencoe, Illinois, went to Hillary Clinton as well. Her gains were nearly as impressive in affluent Republican suburbs, like those edging wests of Kansas City, Missouri, and Houston; north of Atlanta, Dallas and Columbus, Ohio; and south of Charlotte, North Carolina, and Los Angeles, in Orange County. Hillary Clinton didn't always win these affluent Republican enclaves, but she made big gains.

But the narrowness of Hillary Clinton's gains among well-educated voters helped to concentrate her support in the coasts and the prosperous but safely Republican Sun Belt. It left her short in middle-class, battleground-state suburbs, like those around Philadelphia, Detroit and Tampa, Florida, where far fewer workers have a postgraduate degree, make more than $100,000 per year or work in finance, science or technology.

Clinton Failed to Secure the Hispanic Vote

A similar divide may have helped obscure whether Hillary Clinton improved among Hispanic voters. Hillary Clinton was expected to excel among Hispanic voters because of Donald Trump's proposals to deport undocumented workers, his plans to build a wall along the Southern border and his inflammatory comments about Mexican immigrants. The pre-election polls generally showed Hillary Clinton poised to make good on that possibility.

But the election results show a marked decrease in Democratic strength, with Hillary Clinton winning just 66 percent of the Hispanic vote, down from Mr. Obama's 71 percent in 2012. Hillary Clinton plainly fared worse than Mr. Obama in many heavily Hispanic areas — like south Texas or south Colorado. Analysis of election results suggest that she did about the same as Mr. Obama among Hispanic voters over all. The results hint at a potential explanation for why she may have faltered among Hispanic voters without a high school degree while making gains among those with some college education or better.

Nationwide, Hillary Clinton's success in reviving the elements in the caricature version of the Obama coalition really did let her compensate for losses among black voters and working-class whites. She won the popular vote. But she did not do well in the decisive battleground states.

Clinton Underestimated the Silent Majority

Donald Trump's supporters call themselves the "Silent Majority." In an op-ed for Fox News titled "A Loud Cheer for the Silent Majority That Lifted Trump to Victory," Todd Starnes, host of *Fox News & Commentary*, called Trump "a champion for the Silent Majority." He also summed up the values and attitudes of the Silent Majority:

> "It's time to restore traditional values. It's time to protect the Constitution. It's time to defend our sovereignty. It's time to

save unborn babies. It's time to stand up for the American working man and bring jobs back from China and Mexico. It's time to eradicate the scourge of Obama Care. And it's time to hire the bricklayers so they can start building that giant wall."

In June 2016, a Pew Research Center study found a correlation that links negative feelings regarding diversity as well as Islamophobia to "warm feelings" toward Donald Trump. Sixty percent of respondents who believe the growing number of newcomers from other countries threatens U.S. values have warm feelings toward Donald Trump — of which 42 percent have very warm feelings toward him. Of those surveyed overall, 77 percent said they agree that the newcomers threaten American values. In contrast, of those who believe newcomers [strengthen] U.S. society, only 30 percent have warm feelings toward the GOP candidate — compared to 55 percent who have cold feelings.

Implications for Diversity in America

Studies have also shown Donald Trump supporters and voters are less warm regarding diversity issues than Americans overall, particularly when it comes to immigration. Less than half of Trump supporters believe undocumented immigrants are not more likely to commit serious crimes than American citizens, compared to 66 percent of all registered voters. Sixty-six percent of Trump supporters consider immigration a very big problem.

When asked how the United States should effectively deal with illegal immigration, 48 percent said the priority policy should be stronger law enforcement and tightened border security. Just 10 percent said there should be a legal pathway to citizenship for undocumented immigrants, and 41 percent said both policies are important.

For respondents who favored both policies, when asked to choose between the two, 78 percent opted for stronger security and border control, compared to 19 percent who felt a pathway to citizenship was most important. Among Clinton supporters, the results were just about the exact opposite, with 80 percent saying a pathway to citizenship is necessary, compared to 19 percent in favor of security and border protections.

Overall, those who support Trump tend to be less supportive of diversity. The survey asked if having most of the country being black, Asian and Latino — which the census predicts will be the case over the next three decades — is bad for the country or good/neither good nor bad for the country. For respondents who said it's bad, nearly 50 percent report very warm feelings for Trump, with an additional 16 percent saying they have warm feelings. Research has also found that Trump's supporters are more likely to be motivated by racial resentment and hate even when compared to supporters of other Republican candidates.

Chapter 3 —
Analyzing the Postelection Fallout

The politicians' crimes against the country
must be proclaimed and denounced.

Introduction

I sat up for almost two days teary-eyed, reading the stories of men and women all over the country consoling themselves, dealing with the hard outcome of their choice, talking about how they are telling their children of the disappointment that the most qualified presidential candidate couldn't shatter the glass ceiling and then resolving to safeguard each other.

Following the election, parents wrote notes to their children, teachers facilitated conversations in schools, companies provided counseling assistance programs to support employees. Several companies sent memos to their its employees that they have access to mental health care in case they want to talk about the trauma they may be facing because of the results of the election. The nation grieved. At least 50 percent of the people who voted grieved. Almost 46 percent of eligible voters did not vote. They did not feel their vote was important, or they felt they were making hard decisions and decided that they did not care about the outcome.

My twelve-year-old niece wrote a letter to the president asking Donald Trump "not to be so mean." I told my niece that I was sorry and that all we could do was pray. She replied sadly, "You're a diversity expert; you have to do more than pray. You have to go to work and make things better for our country." For the myriad of people committed to affirming a diverse society through nurturing inclusive environments and policies, the election of Donald Trump was devastating. While postmortems are key to lessons learned about the missed chances, the urgency is to regroup so that with strength and wisdom we can be ready to address what lies ahead.

There Ain't No Such Thing as Superman

A combination of factors of manipulations, distortions and external interferences clearly eroded Clinton support: documented voter suppression laws that depressed turnout in key states like Wisconsin and North Carolina, former FBI Director Comey's letters, Russian interference using daily hacked email revelations via WikiLeaks. Any one of these alone could have accounted for enough vote suppression and dampening of enthusiasm to have tipped the election. These alarming realities are indicative that US democracy is fragile enough that it can be susceptible to these types of machinations. They require the most vigorous efforts to double down on protecting the rights of all to vote and to be able to do so with ease as well as the need for urgent investigation into how federal agencies as well as foreign powers interfered in the outcomes of a democratic process.

But we cannot allow these outrageous, unethical and Machiavellian tactics to blind us to the structural reasons that also contributed to Hillary Clinton's loss. Because if we do — for all their egregiousness and recognition that these manipulations did cost Clinton the election — we will miss one of the big important messages of this election.

Before I elaborate on that message, let's name the one message we did hear loud and clear: that Donald Trump's rhetoric — verbatim and through insinuations — gave license to the racists, xenophobes and misogynists to spew unfiltered their hateful beliefs and to even go further through acts of intimidation and fear. To this we

26

only have one response: to expose and to counter. This means we need to not let the public and the media paper over a reality that is instilling deep and real fear on millions of people. While disagreements on public policy should be vigorously debated, when it comes to hate crimes, it must be zero tolerance. This is what will get people to stand up for their rights and/or the rights of others.

At the same time, there is that other message that we must pay attention to: there is a very real and legitimate angst and anger toward our economic system that is leaving way too many behind. This, too, was behind not just Donald Trump's support but also Bernie Sanders's.

So, yes, we can righteously and rightly blame voter suppression, Comey, Julian Assange, the Russians and the haters for manipulating the election results and, in that, tipping the scales in ways that will be unleashing misery, marginalization or worse on so many and along the way erode the very foundations that have made the US in the past an exemplar of democratic ideals of diversity and inclusion.

Must Be Something We Can Do

In exploring the external reasons for Donald Trump's historic win, the first thing I want to say is "Mandate, my ass!" While it's highly likely that manipulations like voter suppression, untimely FBI interference and collusion between the Russian government and WikiLeaks tipped the balance in favor of Trump, we would be doing the work of diversity and inclusion a great disservice if we kept our fingers pointed outward.

There is no place in a pluralistic society for racism, misogyny and the fear and degradation of those who are immigrants, Muslims, LGBTQ or with disabilities, and we must be clear and brave in our condemnation of hate speech and acts. But we must now look in the mirror. Because the deeper structural socioeconomic and cultural

27

societal issues that played out — that was more powerful that the manipulations — was a complete misreading of the mood and realities of working-class and rural whites. And while we must also do the work of finding a way to build bridges with the most intolerant, right here I am focused on a different group of Trump supporters: the ones who voted for Barack Obama two times in a row. In looking at electoral maps of Wisconsin, Michigan and Pennsylvania — states that Obama won in 2008 and 2012 — and comparing them to the 2016 electoral maps, we see a striking reality: there were plenty of rural white areas who voted for an African American president. Therefore, we cannot then ascribe racism as the sole driver for all Trump supporters because racists don't vote for a black man to be their president.

So how can it be that so many of these white rural and working-class voters switched from Obama to Trump? Many will ascribe it to sexism. And I'm sure this was at play for a certain percentage. But where prejudice exists, there is more likely a correlation between not voting for a black man and not voting for a woman than there is a hierarchy of marginalization where a white woman fares worse than a black man in their eyes.

So here is where we need to seek to understand a constituency that too many of those who have embraced diversity and inclusion have frankly stigmatized at worst and not sought to better understand at best.

Over the years, I have worked in places like Cedar Rapids, Iowa; Oshkosh, Wisconsin; and Allentown, Pennsylvania. At the same time, I have also had colleagues and friends from Midwestern states who voted for Donald Trump in 2016. I have sat across from dozens of people in these areas, and we considered each other's eyes, and I can attest to a genuine desire on the part of many of these people for the country to be a pluralistic, diverse and strong nation — the same values and desires those in the country's major cities declare.

We Missed the Whole Point

But here's the part we have often missed: their anxiety has been growing because their world has been underdoing deep, fast and structural changes. The lift and shift of whole factories from these communities to China and Mexico left nothing behind. Overnight, livelihoods and ways of life were obliterated.

There is a direct correlation between these economic dislocations that have led to higher white male unemployment and the rise in depression and from there to the rise in opiate addiction, suicides and now, for the first time ever in generations, a decline in life expectancies among these white working-class and rural populations.

And so, in their bewilderment, they seek answers and are very susceptible to someone coming along and giving them a scapegoat: those who do not look like them. And it is a highly visible scapegoat because, as we all know, those of us in the diversity and inclusion community have been touting these demographic changes for over a decade. These demographic changes are now transforming the face not just of the big cities but also of small towns and rural areas. In small towns that previously had little or no diversity, people channel their anger and anxiety and blame toward those who don't look like them. The result is frightening levels of racism, xenophobia, homophobia and sexism in these communities.

Of course, this is a destructive response. Yet it does not negate their growing sense of despair and their fears that the root causes of it are not being addressed. This phenomenon was also behind the support of someone else who was ideologically opposite to Trump: Bernie Sanders. We must look at the groundswell of support of these two candidates as fueled by some of same root causes even as these

29

two candidates had completely different strategies for channeling the anxiety — with Trump relying on pitting one group against all the others while Sanders was clearly inclusive in intent though nevertheless struggled with bridging the racial divide in linking white and people of color working-class distress. It's a matter of fact that the Sanders movement was not truly racially diverse.

But it was Clinton who had the best opportunity to give some attention to white working-class and rural constituencies. After all, the supposed blue firewall of Pennsylvania, Michigan and Wisconsin had voted Democratic for over thirty years, which included being carried by Barack Obama. Instead, she doubled down, as we tend to do in our diversity and inclusion work, on the traditionally marginalized — women, people of color, LGBT, immigrants — with no outreach to the white working-class and rural populations. How many times did Hillary Clinton go to Wisconsin during the general election? Zero. She lost there by twenty-seven thousand votes.

And in Michigan, where even though the auto industry had been bailed out by Obama, both the distaste of Trump and the feelings of being neglected by Clinton were so deep that there were ninety thousand ballots filled out front and back with selections for all positions to be voted on but that left the presidential nominee option blank. Clinton lost Michigan by fewer than twelve thousand votes.

In other words, if there had been even just a little more focus on white working-class and rural inclusion — without having to give up the messages of inclusion of all the other groups — we would not be blaming the FBI or the Russians or WikiLeaks for the results of the 2016 presidential election. While it's clear these developments tipped the election, they would not have been enough to do so if Clinton's position had not been eroded by these other reasons.

If we say we are about inclusion, then we need to be about inclusion of all. After all, we are all citizens of the same nation with a mutual desire for better lives for our families and communities. So, we have a two-pronged complex challenge before us: on the one hand to be vigilant against the frightening antidiversity forces that have been unleashed and on the other to initially reach into the margins of the Silent Majority and seek common cause.

Moment of Truth

How does the country move on after one of the most bitter, nasty and divisive presidential campaigns in history? How do we become one nation? Invoking the legacy of Abraham Lincoln, Donald Trump promised to heal America's divisions even as he threatened to sue his female accusers and insinuated that the election is rigged. Trump might be ill-suited to serve as "healer in chief." But that does not mean that the country cannot heal itself. Other countries damaged by conflict have tackled the issue of reconciliation and came up with an effective formula.

Several years ago, inspired by the work of the Truth and Reconciliation Commission in South Africa, I made it a point to learn more about the process. What I learned was that reconciliation begins with seeking the truth while acknowledging the grievances of the distressed and providing some way to address the pain caused by the damage.

None of the reconciliation efforts were perfect. Even South Africa's, which became the gold standard, was not nearly as successful as it was originally thought. Although it provided a memorable glimpse of tearful perpetrators apologizing to those they had wronged, most victims received only a fraction of the compensation they had expected, and many never had the satisfaction of seeing the wrongdoers accept responsibility.

Despite the imperfections, the process played an essential role in helping South Africa avoid a descent into unending violence. It also provided a means to begin to address the pain and the conflict of apartheid. South Carolina is not South Africa, where citizens armed by a foreign power brutalized their countrymen and tortured civilians.

Our conflict in America, whether it be in South Philly or South Dakota, is on an altogether different scale, though it is serious enough. According to the Southern Poverty Law Center, the Trump campaign mobilized the crudest alliance of racists, nationalists, nativists, misogynists and angry white men that America has seen in any national election since World War II. The Trump campaign also caused fear and uncertainty in Latino and Muslim communities and anger and resentment — already brought to a boil by police shootings and other tragedies — among blacks. And it drew the wrath of countless women.

The beginning of reconciliation in America, as elsewhere, will be the acknowledgment of the grievances of affected groups — including blue-collar white men, many of whom have been deeply wronged by "the system." Coming back from the brink also entails reconciliation of a different truth. All the pain, anger and resentment stirred up by the 2016 presidential campaign was not created by the Trump campaign. Much of it was present all along, just waiting for a candidate like Donald Trump to set things off.

While our democracy is much too strong to be taken down by 2016 presidential election, it can be deeply damaged by the refusal to acknowledge and address the marginalization and suffering of so many people. Occupy Wall Street, Black Lives Matter, the Bernie Sanders movement, the #MeToo movement and the 2016 presidential campaign all speak to a failure in how America works for many of its less privileged citizens. The challenge of the Trump administration will be not just putting the conflict of the campaign behind us but also addressing those deeper, preexisting needs, if we are to move on to a brighter future.

Implications for Diversity in America

Although Donald Trump won the election, the country has endured months of division that mark a low point in the country's history. So, now what? Rather than indulging in backbiting postmortems on what went wrong, we must try to find a new sense of purpose and unity. Here are few things I think we should try:

First, let's stop demonizing the opposition and those whose viewpoints we don't share. During the relentless presidential campaign of 2016, we heard far more about outrage toward Barak Obama and Hillary Clinton than about visions for a new world. Just as Obama took office, there were a lot of people who expressed a desire to see him fail. Some people even sought to disqualify the former president as an illegitimate usurper through the "birther" campaign or labeled him as a person determined to destroy the country he had been elected to serve. The same tone persisted against Clinton, with ugly chants of "Lock her up!" appealing primarily to the ultra-right-wing of the Republican party. I believe what people want most today is collaboration and progress in Washington. You can't achieve that if you're promising to throw your opponents in jail or labeling them as Satan because of their "evil" intentions.

The next thing that should is happen is that the Trump administration should not make absurd promises that it can't keep.

Chapter 4 —
Voters in Red States Are
Not Barbarians at the Gate

Ain't nobody fighting because nobody knows what to save.

Introduction

Is the white working-class an angry backward monolithic group of 90 million white Americans without college degrees, all standing around with their Bibles and rifles? Most people think so after the 2016 presidential election.

Political analysts have talked about how ignorance, racism, sexism, nationalism, Islamophobia, economic disenfranchisement and the decline of the middle class contributed to the popularity of Donald Trump in rural America. But this misses the deeper cultural factors that shape the thinking of the conservatives who live and work in the "red" states where Trump won the popular vote.

Angels and Aliens

On the Thursday following the 2016 presidential election, I stopped by a neighborhood coffee shop to pick up my usual blend of coffee and favorite pastries. As I was ordering, two young men pushed away from their table, and one said: "Let's go to work. Some of us have to go work and pay taxes so that those people can mooch off the government." The other nodded and they left the coffee shop.

"Those people?" I couldn't resist. I followed the two young men out of the coffee shop — without ordering my much-needed caffeine and sugar — and asked them if they had a few minutes to talk to me. Well, that few minutes turned into almost one hour — I'm sure I made them late for work. I can only hope that I didn't get them into trouble.

What I found out during our conversation was that they are both hard workers. As a kid, Larry had washed dishes, taken orders and swept the floor at a restaurant. Every summer, the other, Martin, had picked sweet corn by hand at dawn for a farm stand and for grocery stores and then went to work all day on his parents' farm. Now Larry is a welder for a large utility company in Atlanta, and Martin is attending Georgia State University. They are both conservative and believe in hard work, loving family, a strong military and tough law enforcement. They both believe that abortion and socialism are evil, that Jesus Christ is their savior and that Donald J. Trump will make America great again.

Larry and Martin are part of a growing movement in rural America that immerses many young people in a culture — not just conservative news outlets but also home and church environments — that emphasizes contemporary conservative values. It views liberals as loathsome, misinformed and weak, even dangerous.

Who are these rural, red-state people who brought Donald Trump into power? I'm a native of Philadelphia, Pennsylvania, and a diversity executive who lives and works in metropolitan Atlanta. I consider myself liberal. My family has voted Democratic since long before I was born. To be honest, for years, even I have struggled to understand how my conservative friends and neighbors I respect — and at times admire — can think so differently from me, not to mention how so many people voted for Donald Trump for president of the United States.

For me, it took a 2016 article in the *New York Times* by J. C. Watts, a Baptist minister raised in the small town of Eufaula, Oklahoma, who was a Republican congressman from 1995 to 2003, to help me begin to understand my Republican colleagues — and most likely other rural Americans as well.

According to Mr. Watts, "the difference between Republicans and Democrats is that Republicans believe people are fundamentally bad, while Democrats see people as fundamentally good. We are born bad and children do not need to be taught to behave badly — they are born knowing how to do that. We teach them how to be good. We become good by being reborn — born again. Democrats believe that we are born good, that we create God, not that he created us. If we are our own God, as the Democrats say, then we need to look at something else to blame when things go wrong — not us."

In the article, Mr. Watts talked about a 2015 movie theater shooting in Lafayette, Louisiana, in which two people were killed. According to Mr. Watts, Republicans knew that the gunman was a bad man doing a bad thing. Democrats, he added, "looked for other causes — that the man was basically good, but that it was the guns, society or some other place where the blame lies and then they will want to control the guns, or something else — not the man. Republicans don't need to look anywhere else for the blame."

Reading the article by Mr. Watts provided an epiphany for me. For the first time, I had a glimpse of where some of my conservative colleagues, friends and neighbors were coming from. I thought, no wonder Republicans and Democrats can't agree on things like gun control, regulations or the value of social programs. We live in different philosophical worlds, with different foundational principles. Overlay this philosophical perspective on the American rural-urban divides of history, economy and geography, and the conservative individual responsibility narrative becomes even more powerful. In my experience, the urban-rural divide isn't so much a red-state-versus-blue-state issue — it's red country versus blue country. Rural Iowans have more in common with the residents of Allentown,

Pennsylvania, and Appleton, Wisconsin — places I've also lived — than with the residents of Philadelphia or Milwaukee.

Look at a national map of which counties went for Democrats and which for Republicans in the 2016 presidential election. Overwhelmingly, the blue counties are along waterways, where early river transportation encouraged the formation of cities and surround state capitals. This is also where most investment in infrastructure and services is made. Rural Americans recognize that this is how it must be, as the cities are where most of the people are, yet it's a sore spot.

In state capitals across America, lawmakers spend billions of dollars to take a few seconds off a city dweller's commute to his office, while rural counties' farm-to-market roads fall into disrepair. Some of the paved roads in rural areas are no longer maintained and are reverting to gravel. For a couple of generations now, services that were once scattered across rural areas have increasingly been consolidated in urban areas, and rural towns die. It's all done in the name of efficiency.

In cities, firefighters and emergency medical technicians are professionals whose departments are funded by local, state and federal tax dollars. Rural America relies on volunteers. If a person has a serious heart attack at home, that person will be dead by the time the volunteer ambulance crew from the town twenty-two miles away gets here. Urban police officers have the latest in computer equipment and vehicles, while small-town cops go begging.

In this view, blue counties are where most of our tax dollars are spent, and that's where all the laws are written and passed. To rural Americans, their taxes mostly go to making city residents' lives better. The truth is more complex, particularly when it comes to social programs, but it's the perception that matters — certainly to the way most people vote.

To make matters worse, jobs are continuing to move to metropolitan areas. Small-town chamber of commerce directors and mayors still have big dreams and use their perkiest grins and tax abatements to try to lure new businesses, only to see their hopes dashed, time and again. Many towns with rich histories and strong community pride are already dead; their citizens just don't know it yet.

Many moderate rural Republicans became supporters of Donald Trump when he released his list of potential Supreme Court nominees who would allow the possibility of overturning Roe v. Wade. They also think the liberal worldview creates unnecessary rules and regulations that cripple the economy and take away good jobs that may belong to them or their neighbor. Red state voters believe that public school systems and colleges are liberal tools of indoctrination that go after what they love and value most: their children.

Some of what liberals worry about is what conservatives see as pure nonsense. When you are the son or daughter of a carpenter or mechanic and a housewife or secretary who lives paycheck to paycheck, who can't afford to send kids to college, as many rural residents are, white privilege is meaningless and abstract.

While many blame poor decisions by Hillary Clinton for her loss, in an environment like this, the Democratic candidate probably didn't matter. And the Democratic Party may not for generations to come. The Republican brand is strong in rural America — perhaps even strong enough to withstand a disastrous Trump presidency.

It's not just older people. The two young men at breakfast exemplify a younger generation with this view. When Ted Cruz campaigned in Macon, Georgia, I watched on television as a couple of dozen grade-school pupils sat at his feet, as if they were at a children's service at church. His campaign speech was nearly a sermon, and the children listened wide-eyed when he told them the world is a scary place, and it's godly men like him who are going to save them from the evils of President Obama, Hillary Clinton and the Democrats.

Rural conservatives feel that their world is under siege and that Democrats are an enemy to be feared and loathed. Given the philosophical premises Mr. Watts presented as the difference between Democrats and Republicans, reconciliation seems a long way off.

The Truth About Trump Voters

Most people attribute the election of Donald Trump to those who are angry, white and working-class; male, conservative, racist, sexist. This description of the people who live in red states and who voted for Donald Trump is inaccurate in several ways. It ignores the people of color, along with progressive white voters. It gives college-educated white liberals a "get out of jail free" card while denying the sin that they too voted for Donald Trump. It conceals well-informed, highly educated white conservatives — from middle-class suburbia — who voted for Donald Trump in the millions.

The trouble begins with labels. The media regularly refers to red state voters as shorthand for right-wing white men wearing NASCAR baseball caps. The truth is most voters in red states are struggling white working-class people who are angrier at their supervisors than their coworkers or neighbors of color. They are angrier about power and privilege than they are about race or immigration. The phrase "Make America Great Again" — in the minds of red state voters — doesn't mean a return to times that were worse for women and people of color but progress toward a society in which everyone can succeed.

Yes, red state voters are angry at someone. They are angry at the companies they work for that they believe exploit workers and they are also angry at the government that they believe punishes the working-class. They consider corporations and government two heads of a capitalist snake that bites people and sucks them dry.

Still, millions of white working-class people have resisted the traps of racism, sexism, homophobia, xenophobia and nationalism and voted the other way — or, in some cases, not voted at all. In fact, the results of 2016 presidential election show in several cases many Wisconsin workers have more in common ideologically with the Democratic Socialists in New York than with the white Republicans in their own state. The political analysts have written a lot about the fact that the white working-class shifted to the right. But Donald Trump won among white college graduates too. Among the thirty states declared "red" after the 2016 presidential election, in two-thirds of them, Hillary Clinton received 35to 48 percent of the vote. Some additional facts that impacted the election outcome but that went basically unreported include: a large minority of white working-class people who were rendered invisible by the Electoral College, unfair barriers to voting, draconian gerrymandering, super PACs that are too big to fail and voter disenfranchisement tactics worthy of only the worst Third World countries.

Let's not forget about the rise of populism on the left. Although populism is often associated with the far right, the 2016 presidential election results revealed that the American left is experiencing a populist resurgence. As a result, progressive congressional candidates with working-class backgrounds and platforms have major support heading into the 2018 midterm Congressional elections and the 2020 presidential election.

Implications for Diversity in America

The debates that have followed the results of the 2016 presidential election have been an inflammatory mix of accusations and counteraccusations. Discussions of root causes and major restructuring of both rural and urban areas have been sporadic at best. Trump supporters can be forgiven for being angry and believing that counties, states, and the federal government have not, or will not allocate the resources required.

Healing a chronic set of race-related circumstances is not America's strong suit. Historically, we have struggled with the long-term political will, material investment and education resources needed to overcome the current economic inequities. Although this has been the case for decades, the election of Donald Trump is an opportunity to better understand the serious issues that exist in America. It's an opportunity to learn from them and — if we don't screw it up — maybe even motivate us do something.

To fully appreciate the diversity of America, we must resist stereotypical narratives about any group. The greatest con of the 2016 presidential election was not persuading a white working-class worker to vote for a billionaire who doesn't care about their interests. Rather, it was persuading the media to cast every working-class American in the same mold. We need to change our way of thinking and talking to voters who just happen to live in a state that voted for Donald Trump. Do we have what it takes? Or will we become the poster child for Abraham Lincoln's famous quote, "A house divided against itself cannot stand"?

Chapter 5 —
The Fall of Civility, Compassion
and Common Sense

And now democracy is ragtime on the
corner hoping for some rain.

Introduction

Since the 2016 presidential election, we have entered uncharted times with the rising neoconservative, white nationalist and racist influence on American society. These forces are seeking to reverse and disturb cultures of inclusion and respectability for all citizens.

Diversity and inclusion are part of the American fabric of life that will not change due to the 2016 presidential election or other political changes. If we study history, we can see similar times and disruptions. The question for the diversity and inclusion professional is "how do we remain relevant during these times and continue our momentum toward a more inclusive society in general and a more respectful climate in our workplaces?"

Clear and Present Danger

The societal changes that we are witnessing because of the 2016 presidential election are not ordinary changes. They are transformational on several levels, and as a result, we are seeing four negative trends begin to emerge that are reshaping the country and forcing diversity professionals to adjust to this new reality.

The first trend that has emerged is that economic conditions and environmental concerns (climate change, loss of jobs, migration, hunger, war) have forced people in many parts of the country to mi-grate to areas of increased security and safety. People want to earn livable wages and to ensure stability within their own families. When threats to survival increase, individuals become more hostile to difference and fear increases. Equitable outcomes and success are impacted by conditions of life that go beyond race and gender. These take on an immediacy that increases the impact of historical bias and discrimination against certain groups. We can see this in the grow-ing concern by working-class white males who feel left out of the diversity and inclusion conversation. To many of them, diversity and inclusion initiatives create "winners and losers," and they see themselves being left out economically. Poverty, socioeconomic status, education and other conditions are having an adverse effect on the ability of working-class people to compete on a "level playing field."

The second trend that is emerging and creating a clear and pre-sent danger to diversity and inclusion efforts is the demographic ex-plosion in many areas, especially urban centers. This explosion is changing the political and social dynamic and reinforcing fear, par-ticularly among working-class whites. This fear is creating a counter movement intent on mitigating the impact to their privilege and his-torical preference. Factual arguments are giving way to biblical and identity-based opposition to women, people of color and Muslims and immigrants, fostering a desire for greater homogeneity and that use false narratives to reinforce perspectives. The objective of such suppositions is to destroy beliefs and values supportive of inclusion by distorting, twisting and bending the truth. This behavior and re-sponse also can be found in social media and other forums where explicit attempts to mischaracterize, falsify and even pervert rules are used. Some are deliberately behaving in disrespectful, unacceptable ways that are contrary to accepted standards of civility or compassion.

The third trend that is emerging and threatening to derail efforts to bring about a more diverse and inclusive society is the rapid acceleration of conscious bias. The demographic shift is resulting in an unprecedented growth in people of color, especially immigrants and Hispanics, and has helped to kick-start a movement to reverse the demographic trends that are felt to have a disproportionate impact on the opportunities and preferences for working-class whites. Unconscious and sometimes conscious bias are emerging to foster a desire to eliminate, impede, reverse and discount the challenges and legitimacy of institutional racism and systemic barriers to societal inclusion. White nationalist extremists are working to turn back the clock on affirmative action and diversity and are obliged to prevent diversity views from being heard or considered. Those of us in the diversity and inclusion profession refer to this as "diversity genocide."

The fourth trend that is creating headwinds and threatening to slow the progress of diversity and inclusion efforts is that economic activity is shifting the locus of its activities to emerging markets, which are mainly in urban centers. Population growth in these urban centers is significant and is becoming more diverse with many of these urban centers in the US becoming majority-minority centers. Nearly half of the national GDP growth between 2016 and 2020 will come from forty cities in these emerging markets, according a McKinsey study. In the 2016 presidential election, a lot of attention was paid to these centers by Democratic candidates without comparable attention to rural America. Given the fear in the minds of many working-class whites, it is easy to see how much of the more rural working-class whites supported Trump. This rural-urban divide will be a challenge to the aspiration of a unified America as more working-class whites gravitate to nationalism and populism influence.

Perhaps one of the most impactful trends is the accelerating pace of technological change. Many working-class individuals, regardless of their race, have seen a rapid and steady decline in manufacturing jobs, particularly in rural communities. In some urban centers, there has also been significant job loss. Most working-class people attribute the decline to jobs moving to other countries. While this is true to some degree, the major contributor to the rapid rate is technological change. Companies are seeing an unprecedented acceleration in the scope, scale, and economic impact of technology. Computer processing power and connectivity are part of the story, but the data revolution is placing unprecedented amounts of information in the hands of consumers and businesses alike. As a result, traditional jobs and apprenticeship programs are being retooled to focus on science, technology, engineering and math skills. Manual skills are being automated, making traditional blue-collar jobs and career paths obsolete. Many working-class whites chose these paths in the '70s and '80s and now find these positions disappearing in record numbers, because of technological innovation. This job loss has increased fear among blue-collar workers, and unskilled and lower-paying jobs are being automated. Many working-class whites are feeling threatened by competition from a more diverse labor pool, which includes significantly more immigrant labor.

Another trend that is raising concern and resulting in backlash against diversity and inclusion efforts is the aging of the population and the workforce. The country's population is getting older, and fertility rates are falling, especially among whites. Simply put, the country's population is graying dramatically; however, the patterns are reversed for Hispanics and Asians. For the first time in 109 years, the country's fertility rates for whites is below those needed to replace the generation before. This rapid decline in birth rates is causing alarm in some white nationalist sectors, which see the country as becoming more mixed-race and with significantly more power shifting to people of color.

Last, but certainly not least, is the trend showing a growing number of people who have unfavorable views about immigration. The United States cannot build a wall and keep out the growing connectedness of people and businesses from around the world. The world is much more connected through trade and through the movement of capital, people and information. The world trading hubs have expanded into a complex, intricate, sprawling web. More than 1 billion people creased borders in 2009, over five times the number in 1980. We are moving from an industrial revolution to a more connected, networked and shared global economy. Industrial ownership is not just American-based but global, with many companies doing business in the US having headquarters outside the US. The cry to stop immigration, to build a wall, to restrict the flow of global talent runs counter to an evolving new world. This networked economy places a higher premium on inclusive leadership, diverse connections, cross-cultural competence and international collaboration.

Implications for Diversity in America

These emerging trends are significant and cannot be dismissed or overlooked. It requires diversity professionals like me to do a lot of soul searching and hard work. We need to realize that much of what we think we know about how more diverse and inclusive companies and communities work is outdated. We need to get a handle on the disruptive forces transforming the country because of the 2016 presidential election and analyze the impact of these emerging mega-standing trends. We need to develop the courage and foresight to clear the intellectual decks and prepare a response. There is a powerful human tendency to want the future to look much like the past. On these shoals, huge corporate vessels have floundered. Revisiting our assumptions about the country we live in — and doing nothing — will leave many people highly vulnerable. Gaining a clear-eyed perspective on how to negotiate the changing landscape will help us prepare to succeed.

Chapter 6 —
Our Communities: More Diverse, More Segregated and Less Inclusive

Now, more than ever, all the family must come together.

Introduction

US cities are rapidly becoming more diverse, but that doesn't mean they are more inclusive. In fact, in many large metro areas, some minority groups are now more segregated from white populations than before, according to an analysis of new US census data by the Brookings Institution. Minorities are driving population growth in large metropolitan areas — they've accounted for 98 percent of it since 2000, per Brookings demographer William Frey, who crunched five-year estimates from the American Community Survey. That is quickly shifting the racial and ethnic makeup of US cities.

A House Divided

The growing proportion of people of color is not spreading evenly throughout cities. Neighborhoods where average white people live, for example, are in general much less diverse than the cities in which they sit. As a result, despite their expanding numbers, people of color in many cities remain deeply isolated from white people.

Segregation of black and white people, for example, has only improved slightly since 2000 as measured by a dissimilarity index. The index's average for the forty-nine metro areas fell by three points to a reading of sixty for the 2011–2015 period. That means that 60 percent of black residents would have to move to be fully integrated with white residents.

Meanwhile, Hispanic communities in twenty-two out of fifty metro areas became more, not less, impoverished as the share of white residents dropped. The all-metro average index for Hispanic-white segregation increased slightly, to forty-eight in 2011–2015 from 47 in 2000. But the jump was much higher in some places, such as the Cincinnati area, where the index increased the most out of all the metro areas Frey looked at.

To be sure, the Hispanic share of Cincinnati's population is tiny, just 3 percent. But segregation also grew in places where Hispanics make up a much bigger proportion of residents.

Inclusion Disruptors Increasing Segregation in Metro Areas

Statistics raise a troubling question about the prospects of patching up the deep racial divisions exposed by the 2016 presidential election: if people living in the same city can't comingle, how can we expect to bridge the divides between rural and urban, between coastal and Midwestern and between Americans of different races and ethnic backgrounds?

Achieving a society that is not only more diverse but also more inclusive will require the country to overcome several hurdles. First among these obstacles is the fact that the population of our urban centers will continue to shift to majority-minority populations in dozens of cities. Identity patterns are changing as people claim multiple identities. The socialist-capitalist challenge will grow as income inequality widens. Twenty-first-century workers will become more self-reliant, networked and multicultural.

Added to this challenge is the fact that as more working-class white Americans feel threatened by the changes promised by diversity and inclusion, there will be growing intolerance of perceived disparate impact and treatment. The demographic change occurring will also create a tipping point around privilege and power. It will also accelerate the shift and balance of power exclusively held by whites. Millennial activists will return to grassroots organizing and nonviolent protests. However, more white nationalists will begin to more openly challenge diversity, inclusion and multiculturalism on several levels including individual, organizational and governmental.

As immigration increases and as people from different religious and cultural backgrounds become a part of the fabric of American society, several trends will emerge. First, cultural and religious polarities will rise, especially when white nationalism, founded in fundamentalist Christian values, conflict with alien and unfamiliar perspectives. Increased immigration will challenge diversity efforts as citizens voice concerns over safety, liberty and freedoms. With more racial integration and mixing, cultural identity and expression will become blurred. And retaliatory acts against immigrants and those with different religious perspectives and nonwhite ethnic identities will become more commonplace if not kept in check.

Implication for Diversity in America

Valuing diversity and fostering inclusion are important to the continuous prosperity of communities and companies on the personal, organizational and structural levels. Diversity professionals must be ever vigilant in their efforts to create more inclusive workplaces and societies. Incremental change will not suffice. We must work at transformational and disruptive change. We must retain a sense of urgency — decisions today are important. The real question is whether the role of money in politics will allow us to continue in a forward direction. Fostering inclusion and valuing diversity should be based on a good understanding of the systemic and disruptive forces needed to bring about social change from Strawberry Mansion to Silicon Valley. These forces include polarities — those for progress and those against it.

The impact must not only consider the narrower dimensions of this work but the economic, subversive and reactionary implications for broader diversity and increased inclusion. Diversity and inclusion are a must for many but a threat to some who want to sustain privilege. The Trump administration appears intent on reversing progress that has been made. I believe that diversity professionals must lead the response that is strong and respectful but unrelenting in the quest for more inclusive companies, communities and, yes, country.

Chapter 7 —
Donald, Dissonance, Disruption
and the Diversity Apocalypse

The character and conduct of this
nation have never looked blacker.

Introduction

As we count the months since that fateful day November 2016, many of us struggle with how we put the pieces back together and move forward as one country with many voices, faces and legacies. Some may dismiss the figures of speech used by Donald Trump as common "political tropes." But others see incredibly tainted and damaging language in speeches and debates, filled with both coded and blatant references to race, stereotypes of communities of color, immigrant scapegoating and divisive suggestions of isolation, barriers and "otherness."

The Sum of All Our Fears

In June 2017, I delivered a keynote address at the Equal Employment Opportunity Commission's Excel Conference in Chicago, and I am still haunted by a question I was asked while delivering my presentation.

As I often do when I speak, I solicit questions during the presentation instead of waiting until the Q&A portion as a way of inviting engagement throughout the conversation. When I solicited the audience for questions at this conference, a woman named Janet raised her hand and asked a question I'm not sure I ever really answered. Paraphrased, to the best of my recollection, Janet's question went something like this: "I'm a white woman, and I have a white son, and I'm afraid for him when I think about what diversity has done to this country. Doesn't this country already have enough diversity?"

While the rest of the audience fidgeted nervously at Janet's transparency and boldness, I recognized Janet's question as a gift. Janet's question pointed to the disservice many diversity practitioners have done to the conversation around diversity and inclusion. For far too long, we have relegated the diversity and inclusion conversation to an optics game, "counting people rather than making people count." And, in our attempts to advance this conversation, well-intentioned as we may have been, we have left out the white men who comprise most leadership in corporate America.

For our attempts at building a truly inclusive company, culture and country to be effective, we must reframe the dialogue around diversity. Diversity is not so much about how one looks but rather about how one thinks. Therefore, what the real goal of diversity and inclusion in corporate America should be about is recognizing and rewarding the constructive disruption that leads to innovation and new ways of thinking. The real currency of the twenty-first century is in ideas, and far too many organizations reward loyalty and punish constructive dissent.

While women, people of color and underrepresented talent in general pay a disproportionate penalty in whether their voices are heard, this is not an organizational dynamic from which white men are completely immune. The evidence around the business value of diversity is irrefutable. In fact, a McKinsey study released in 2017 concluding that more diverse workforces perform better financially is just one of many that point to the bottom-line impact of diversity. McKinsey used the term "diversity dividend" to point to the evidence that companies that are in the top quartile for gender diversity perform better than their competitors and companies that are in the top quartile for ethnic diversity are 35 percent more likely to outperform their peers in the industry. It is important to note here that diversity in and of itself has no value unless inclusion goes hand in hand. It's one thing to have diverse perspectives around your table; it's a whole different dynamic to ensure those diverse perspectives are effectively heard and leveraged for organizational impact. One of my favorite metaphors that illustrates this concept nicely is the following: "Diversity is being invited to the party. Inclusion is being asked to dance."

But perhaps Janet's fear for her son strikes at a much more basic human level. Her question was motivated by a PowerPoint slide that I showed earlier in my presentation that indicated huge demographics shifts in the country based on the latest census. These shifts are largely around the tremendous growth of the Asian, Hispanic and African American populations in this country. What I saw in Janet's question was the fear that leads Janet and so many others to see diversity as a problem and not the opportunity that it truly is. Fear is what leads people to view diversity as a zero-sum game where some must win while others lose. The reality is that diversity presents a huge untapped opportunity. Done correctly, truly inclusive institutions can realize increased market share, create organizational cultures where there are no barriers to great ideas and position themselves well to outperform their competition. But we must get past fear. And so, many voices in our communities and in our companies, point to fear of difference. It explains in part the election of Donald Trump as president in what is arguably one of the most diverse nations on earth. Diversity has been, and always will be, a fact of American life. In fact, over 50 percent of one-year-olds in this country are multicultural, which points to the growth of diversity for a long time to come.

Janet is not very different from many of us in that we are comforted by our uniformity, but we only learn from diversity of perspective. There is growing research that shows that many Americans do not have a close personal relationship with anybody outside their race. Such data showing the irony of being a diverse country yet living in such segregated communities should be troubling to anybody who believes in the true value of diversity. And perhaps there has never been a more urgent call to create connection and hope across difference. If we are to prosper and build a truly inclusive, civil society, we must start creating environments that are safe and respectful of difference. If we do this in a way that impacts not only people of color but also white men, we reframe the diversity dialogue in a way that truly benefits us all.

Without Remorse

In describing the mood of the country after the 2016 presidential election, people have used language like "corrosive," "unhinged" and "unearthed" to describe some of the ways in which we have seen civility and empathy disappear. What many of us do agree on is that things have changed. The discourse has changed, our trust in others has changed and many people are grappling with how to have difficult conversations about what the most nuanced and complex topics of race and identity.

After the 2016 presidential election, more than 40 percent of American voters reported that that they felt despondent, disgusted and betrayed, which is why across the country there are citizen-led efforts underway to heal the divides created by the 2016 presidential election, to repair the social fabric, to restore trust and civility.

We will need to be intentional in how we move forward after 2016 presidential election and how we address issues of race, power and the impact of race/racism in our cities, schools and workplaces.

There is no expiration date on understanding our racial history. It will always be with us.

Talking about race in the US has never been easy and is often viewed as divisive. Our complicated, painful and often undiscussed history around race has created barriers to crucial conversations. Even more difficult for some is the idea of talking about race in the workplace. The vitriol and bigotry that were at the center of the 2016 presidential election has had a documented impact on numerous communities — think Charlottesville, Virginia. Why would we think that it has not impacted us as employees or our workplaces?

In many ways, it appears that colleges and universities have moved ahead of companies and organizations in how they are helping their students deal with some of the impacts of the 2016 presidential election. Discussions facilitated by diversity experts have helped students address their potential biases and understand concepts of power, privilege, access, history, systemic racism and civil discourse. Perhaps companies could learn something from these classroom lessons.

Recent tragedies in our country — following the 2016 presidential election, where implicit bias, race and racism were contributing factors — are frequent and have raised the need for companies to move beyond a narrative of colorblindness, postracial confusion and silence. "Tolerance is for cowards" was the phrase Randall Stephenson, AT&T's CEO, used when talking about the need for real dialogue on race relations. A video of Stephenson calling for a dialogue on race has been shared widely via social media. It is another important example of how we can talk about race in the workplace — and the need to do more. Stephenson's comments came the same week that we saw new research from LeanIn.org and McKinsey about women of color being the most underrepresented group in the corporate workforce.

There is not an impenetrable wall that keeps race-related issues out of the workplace. July 2016 was a time that I can remember when the realities of race and racism have been catalysts for dialogue in the workplace. The pain, anger and confusion surrounding the killings of Philando Castile and Alton Sterling could not be ignored by companies. These events, followed by the tragic killing of two Dallas police officers, highlighted systemic tensions, challenges, biases and need for action that many have not wanted to see. For example, a CBS/*New York Times* poll taken right after the incidents in July 2016 showed America's race relations to be at a low point.

Since the 2016 presidential election, many companies have struggled with crafting messages that would be "sensitive" and responsive to the many fears and concerns that were present in the workplace. Many chief diversity officers came together to share strategies for how they were working toward continued dialogue and action. Many of my colleagues realized that their organizations lacked the awareness, language and skills needed to have an honest conversation about race in the United States and in the workplace. However, many companies did find ways to respond constructively and dedicate time and space for honest conversations. Some held dialogues; some organized roundtables with their CEO; and some organizations conducted town hall meetings on site with employees.

There are countless stories that did not make the news of authentic corporate leaders who set aside meeting agendas to allow space for people to talk about how they were feeling. Following the 2016 presidential election, organizations that had not discussed or acknowledged racial issues or the impact of societal events on employees and the workplace started conducting "crucial conversations" training. The 2016 presidential election provided a catalyst that challenged assumptions of competence, confidence and comfort with diversity in the workplace. For example, candid conversations about race in the workplace would mean that organizations would need to discuss systemic issues of access, privilege, power and more. It would require more engaged and nuanced conversations that move beyond the popular (and yet important) unconscious bias/implicit bias awareness to conversations that address social-economic disparity, with a goal of action and change.

This is part of the deeper conversation that needs to take place. A recent *Harvard Business Review* article, "We Just Can't Handle Diversity," explored some of the challenges with diversity and suggested that awareness of systemic unfairness is part of the challenge with diversity: "If those in power think this world is basically fair and just, they won't even recognize — much less worry about — systemic unfairness."

Not talking about race has prevented many employees in organizations from connecting, understanding each other and learning more about how we can in fact truthfully address the impact of race in companies and communities. My hope is that the 2016 presidential election will propel us to begin to move slowly toward healthier, bolder and honest dialogue — one that cannot just happen after a tragedy or big news story. We cannot undo what we have seen and heard since the 2016 presidential election. But we can acknowledge that the biased statements and continued tragedies will not go away and that we do indeed bring our fears and biases into the workplace. Because of the 2016 presidential election, we need to work even harder to move forward. We cannot mute the conversation about race, sexual harassment and identity in the workplace.

Into the Storm

Another question that I was asked during the Excel 2017 Conference in Chicago came from a man named Jim. He asked me:

"How do you anticipate that a Trump presidency will impede efforts to increase diversity at all levels in corporate America?" My response to Jim was that, despite the widespread pessimistic mood in the country, "it will not." I added, "In fact, it might drive advances in diversity in companies." My answer was based in part on the fact that I believe the problem is not a political one, and the solutions are, and always have been, in the hands of the corporate leaders, whether these leaders are the CEOs of public companies, the leadership team of successful private companies or the founders of tiny start-ups. Yes, there are societal issues underpinning the lack of diversity, but the 2016 presidential election will not move us backward. A I discussed in my previous book, *Crisis as a Platform for Social Change from Strawberry Mansion to Silicon Valley*, it is clearly within the power of companies to promote inclusion and increase diversity.

Frankly, the private sector has zero excuses in terms of where it is today with its widespread lack of diversity. (You can't blame that on the election of Trump!) Going forward, it will continue to have zero excuses, whoever is in the White House. But perhaps the shock of the 2016 presidential election will encourage corporate leaders to increase their efforts to improve diversity. Why? First, the three-legged business case is still there, and unless companies seek out the best talent, they will never have the best teams they can have, because diverse talent is equally distributed but equal opportunity is not. Second, diversity is the catalyst for innovation and hence is vital to winning in any competitive marketplace. Third, US companies dominate most global industries because they have diverse teams who, when fully appreciated and leveraged, capture most market opportunities. And only with diverse teams will companies have an employee profile to support their global brands. Lastly, the 2016 presidential election has made the moral case even stronger. Healing wounds in society and "doing the right thing" take on a new urgency — I expect many corporate leaders will respond to that call.

Implications for Diversity in America

While I was conducting a webinar discussing the implications of the 2016 presidential election, one participant suggested that people of color are feeling more vulnerable now than ever and asked me, "What do companies need to be doing differently to support people of color, Latinos, immigrants, women and the LGBTQ community?" I responded that "we all need to be more open, more engaged, show empathy and crucially listen more. And that doesn't just include the groups you mention. It must include the groups you don't mention, so listening to the voices of people you don't normally talk to, and who clearly felt Trump had a message for them that they responded to positively. And they deserve to be heard, because they and others elected Donald Trump as the president of the United States."

Two months after the election, I participated in a town hall meeting in Milwaukee where the major topic was the election and what to do next. I got one of the best questions from a high school student who had just voted in her first election. She asked me, "Do you anticipate that corporate leaders will move more toward working with a Trump administration or move toward building social justice outside of their companies? Where do you think their efforts will be more effective?" I answered her by saying: "Companies have to do both. Larger companies have interests in tax, social, trade and many other policy areas and have the lobbying machines that give them a voice in policy setting and legislation, and many of the leaders have their bully pulpit too, as public figures."

I went on to explain that President Obama's administration was not seen as corporation-friendly, because he was perceived as too cozy with organized labor and the unions. Now we are in an environment where policy could shift in a direction perceived to be more favorable to business. Companies must and will make their opinions heard. To the point about building social justice outside the walls of the company, corporate leaders also have done that before. For example, many of them spoke out against legislation hostile to the LGBTQ community and likely will do more going forward. However, corporate leaders can be accused of being inconsistent, if not outright hypocritical, in ways that can undermine their legitimacy as a voice for social justice. For example, why were so many of them so vocal on legislation impairing LGBTQ rights but not standing up in the same way against legislation restricting voter rights for people of low income and people of color? And on the hypocrisy front, just look at the demographics of the board of directors and the senior leadership teams of larger companies. These facts alone mean that, for now, corporate leaders lack the high ground from which to adopt a superior position. So, if corporate leaders want to take that high ground on social justice issues, they need to get their act together internally first and in areas they touch directly. Again, they have zero excuses, and there is still so much work to do. Bottom line: necessary future internal actions companies will take will have nothing to do with who is in the White House.

The question that we all need to be asking as we have crucial conversations with each other is "How can we work together going forward?" As a diversity professional who has dedicated years to helping create inclusive work environments where all employees are valued, respected and engaged, I believe we need to start by encouraging and supporting others and sharing best practices to build inclusive and diverse organizations. As one of the candidates in the election was fond of saying: "Do all the good you can, by all the means you can, in all the ways you can, in all the places you can, at all the times you can, to all the people you can, if ever you can."

Chapter 8 —
Conscious Inclusion: The Role of
White Males in the Postelection Era

Great streams are not easily turned from channels,
worn deep during the ages.

Introduction

As we all know (and have felt), the 2016 presidential campaign was incredibly divisive along the lines of gender, education and ethnicity. The spike in the number of hate crimes immediately following the election demonstrates how deep the fractures go in our society and how exclusion — from economic opportunity or by a hyper-focus on diversity — is being deeply felt and experienced by so many. The inevitable, and uncomfortable, conclusion is that many of us were not aware of, or didn't prioritize, full inclusion — in our companies, in our communities and in our country. Given this collective blind spot, and the new reality of the Trump administration, what will companies, communities and the country do differently if we truly believe in the transformative power of valuing differences? The need for inclusiveness is greater than ever.

Debt of Honor

Those of us in the diversity and inclusion profession focus every day on reaching out, and beyond, to those on the margins of our efforts; in the LGBTQ community, this means a focus on "straight allies" as champions willing to put their skin in the game on others' behalf. This forms an alliance with people and communities who feel unsafe or targeted, and it can be very simple to show solidarity.

63

But as someone who focuses on awakening change-makers in companies and communities, I am reminded now more than ever of the opportunity to better engage my white, male colleagues in a different way. Heavily represented in leadership in most organizations, their involvement in building bridges — most importantly, to other men — is critical. It's time to double down and invite them to be partners in our efforts to ensure that all employees feel welcomed, valued, respected and heard in the workplace. Efforts to create and maintain inclusive environments are often being stifled by the perceived tension between the qualifications of diverse employees and the organization's commitment to diversity. Savvy leaders do not ignore or exaggerate the value of diversity; they lead with due regard for the way diversity operates in their relationships and sphere of influence. This is one way all leaders can build trust.

A couple of years ago, Bill Proudman, founder of White Men as Full Diversity Partners, conducted an in-depth leadership survey on white men involved in diversity and inclusion efforts within their respective organizations. Bill Proudman surveyed 670 leaders, 58 percent of whom were white men, and asked them ninety-four diversity- and inclusion-related questions and discovered the following:

- White men possess more than 40 percent of the leadership jobs in most companies, and that percentage increases dramatically by leadership level. The position, power and privilege that white men possess need to align with the value that diversity and inclusion delivers.
- White male leaders are less engaged with their organization's diversity and inclusion than their nonwhite colleagues. As such, they represent a significantly underperforming asset in every company's D&I investment portfolio.

- White men bring their own safety concerns to diversity discussions, and their nonwhite colleagues may wonder if white male inclusion will open doors for everyone. Almost 80 percent of all respondents rated white male managers highly on the ability to show respect for nonwhite coworkers. In contrast, only 36 percent of white male respondents rated white male leaders positively for saying just what needs to be said (candor) among nonwhite coworkers.

Comfort, Confidence and Competence

We're asking white men to change what is a relatively comfortable workplace culture for them, as well as to become voracious students of other cultures, experiences and insights. What they learn in becoming students of these cultures doesn't always cast a flattering light on white men as leaders in general. But they don't share all the burden; one survey respondent said, "I feel like we, as white men, are the forgotten group in the company, when it comes to diversity and inclusion." Exclusion is a powerful disincentive, and if white men imagine that they have been shut out of the inclusion conversation — and they do, even now — it is more difficult to create and sustain inclusive organizations. Every member of an underrepresented community has felt excluded many, many times; exclusion is more universal than we know. Can white leaders harness the sense that they have?

White Males as Full Diversity Partners

In some organizations, the terms "diversity" and "white men" are treated as mutually exclusive. White men often report feeling left out of their organizations' diversity and inclusion initiatives, which can result in anger, confusion or indifference toward these

65

diversity and inclusion initiatives. My good friend and diversity expert Bill Proudman encourages candid dialogue to overcome the "white guy equals bad guy" stereotype. In fact, Proudman suggests that the important thing is for organizations to engage white males in a conversation about their experiences with diversity. He contends that it is important to provide white males and others with the chance to learn more about the norms that have dominated white male behavior and influenced many corporate cultures.

Because only a handful of companies have had the insight and courage to appoint a white man to head up the organization's diversity department, empirical research on the link between this practice and organizational performance is missing from the literature. Based on my experience, this issue is important to get diversity management initiatives off the sidelines and into the mainstream of the business. Encouraging white men to champion diversity efforts — particularly those who work in the core business lines and operations — can help bring other white males on board as full partners in the organization's diversity and inclusion efforts.

Women and people of color and other underrepresented groups do not have the power and influence to effect change in largest organizations; therefore, the senior leaders in the organization must recognize the critical role that white men play in organizational change. Proudman, the founder and president of White Men as Full Diversity Partners, suggests that any diversity and inclusion initiative that does not engage white men by showing them that they will benefit from the initiative is doomed to fail. In fact, if white men are not present at the table when the diversity strategy is conceived they will not be fully committed to or genuinely supportive of the strategy or the desired outcomes.

There is plenty of research that points out that some diversity and inclusion initiatives make white men feel defensive — take bias training, for example. The remedy to this dilemma is for organizations to take intentional actions to engage white men in the organizations' diversity efforts. Organizations will find it very difficult to sustain their diversity efforts if white men think that there is nothing in it for them. Therefore, organizations should start by helping white male managers gain a deeper understanding of diversity management and its relationship to the organizations' business goals. This is best accomplished by emphasizing that diversity and inclusion initiatives (e.g., diversity training) can help them create a more inclusive work environment and effectively manage high-performing diverse work teams.

White Males as Diversity Champions

I believe that it would be beneficial if more chief diversity officers were white men who came out the core operations side of business. However, the research suggests that for the first time in their lives, white males are worrying about their future opportunities because of widespread layoffs and corporate restructuring. As a result, white men are feeling threatened because of organizational efforts to increase racial, ethnic and gender representation. This fear is, in part, a new manifestation of the old backlash against affirmative action. At the heart of the issue for many white males is the question of merit. In other words, as organizations pursue the goal for a more diverse workplace, white males believe they will lose out to nonwhites and females.

Although this is an old argument that has little empirical foundation or support in the research, experts believe that it has been a powerful deterrent for some white men who believe that an assignment as chief diversity officer will derail their career. This is an important issue that has been overlooked by most organizations in the development of their diversity management strategies. This oversight can be mostly attributed to the fact that organizations believe that the business case for diversity and inclusion initiatives is not legal, as it is with affirmative action, but rather economic (i.e., in terms of "competitiveness" and "viability"). Consequently, this results in the belief that diversity management initiatives will be accepted unconditionally by white males, unions and even white male managers.

But as organizations are seeing the nationwide assault against race- and gender-based employment programs, this has not been the case. The tepid support of diversity and inclusion initiatives on the part of white males stems from organizations' failure to address the concerns of white men about the effects of policies and programs aimed at promoting nonwhites and females. As a result, organizations will need to work with white males so that they understand that diversity goals are based on inclusion, not exclusion. Moreover, diversity leaders must emphasize that organization diversity and inclusion initiatives do not seek to displace white males but rather to prepare employees and managers to work in a trusting and inclusive work environment — one where everyone is valued, respected and engaged — to help organizations achieve long-term, sustainable success. Diversity initiatives should go beyond race, gender, ability and age to cover, for example, career development planning for everyone. I believe that organizations will be challenged by a critical dilemma as they address the needs and concerns of white males. They assert that organizations must not ignore the concerns of white women and people of color, who may resent efforts to win over or pamper white males.

Implications for Diversity in America

Common sense suggests that having white male voices dedicated to the goals of diversity and inclusion is critical to long-term, sustainable success of organizations. Some diversity and inclusion experts suggest that appointing white men as chief diversity officers is counterintuitive and that employees in affected organizations will question their qualifications. While divided on several aspects of this issue, most experts agree that the onus is on white men to show that they are truly committed to creating a diverse workforce and that their efforts to make sure diversity and inclusion initiatives include white males do not come at the expense of sacrificing the larger agenda. Have white men been left behind long enough to begin to imagine what others have experienced routinely?

White men can learn to accept and invite difference; the rest of us need to find a way to include the white men in our diversity efforts without sublimating ourselves. The leaders who will successfully adjust must embrace discomfort and address their own possible misperceptions that they are under threat. In short: they must become "comfortable with being uncomfortable." That, as I see it, is the only way forward...for all of us.

Chapter 9 —
The Workplace as a Healing Space

Common blood flows through common veins,
and common eyes all see the same.

Introduction

CEOs have been calling me since the bombshell results of the 2016 presidential election. They seek a sounding board for how best to respond as leaders of their organizations. They know that inside their corporate, store, plant and factory walls flow the full crosscurrents of polarized employees stoked by poisonous rhetoric. But they are unsure of how best to lead in these dangerous times. Do they just hope that employees will keep their thoughts and feelings to themselves while they are at work? They quickly recognize this "head in the sand" approach will not be sustainable nor helpful, but they hesitate to encourage the alternative of inviting expression from people across a wide political spectrum out of understandable fear that this would only devolve into mirroring the rancor on the streets, cable news and social media.

A Crisis Is a Terrible Thing to Waste

A survey conducted in August 2017 — nine months after the 2016 presidential election — by the American Psychological Association found that one in four US employees reported being negatively affected by political discussion at work, with younger workers especially reporting diminished productivity and increased stress.

70

And many employees reported feelings distanced from their colleagues and having more negative feelings toward them, as well as an uptick in workplace hostility, all due to political conversations.

A Gallup survey conducted soon after the election found that more than 25 percent of respondents said that they anticipate negative impact on productivity in their workplaces. Another 43 percent said they are undecided or just don't know what the overall impact might be; this uncertainty surely contributes to a degree of distraction as well.

In April 2018, I spoke at the SHRM Atlanta SOAHR Conference, and the personal stories and observations shared by conference participants I spoke to reflect these themes:

"The election has definitely impacted workforce productivity. Suddenly there is confusing guidance or lack of clarity on the practical applications of several employment laws. The new administration has created a tremendous amount of work. It has heightened anxiety across a huge population of employees who don't know how they will be impacted by changes in immigration, health care, etc. It has created distraction," noted a participant.

"The 2016 presidential election has created uncertainty for our employees and job candidates with nonimmigrant work visa status, which serves as a distraction," said another conference participant.

And: "Those who are not directly impacted by pending changes have expressed that they have family members who are impacted, close and distant. This causes added stress to their lives affecting health and well-being. Others who are reminded of their immigrant experience have more empathy for the plight of current immigrants and refugees. The sense of helplessness and frustration in our company is palpable."

Almost everyone agrees that in the months following the 2016 presidential election, the country has collectively experienced subtle and not-so-subtle social changes that unavoidably carry over into the workplace.

We are witnessing the emergence of a growing community of dissenters; protests, rallies and other public demonstrations are regular occurrences. There have been calls for a nationwide strike. Organizers of the Women's March on Washington have announced plans for future protests. Other national days of demonstration include a protest of the repeal of Obama Care and a Tax Day March.

In general, we seem to be more tuned in to what is happening and clearly consuming more news. The *New York Times* reported record growth in readership, adding 276,000 digital-only subscribers in the first quarter of 2017 alone. Cable and network news viewership is up as well. And if it's possible, we're checking our Twitter accounts even more frequently than usual. But all this close attention to the latest news updates, tweets or alerts feels like a Groundhog Day–like loop of waiting for the other shoe to drop (and there are an immeasurable number of shoes). It isn't helping most employees feel more positive or productive. More likely, we are exhausted and a little depressed by it all.

Recipe for Healing

As a diversity professional who has dedicated almost two decades to helping leaders manager diverse work teams and create inclusive work places, I offer some thoughts of what CEOs and other business and D&I leaders can do to right now to help provide safe spaces for dialogue and healing. After all, the workplace is where people spend most of their waking time, and given the uniqueness of a group of people connected by a common commercial, and in certain places, community, purpose, there is an opportunity to take advantage of this unique context to offer a political DMZ where a different type of dialogue can take place.

Lead Inclusively: Leaders should acknowledge that the concerns of all parties are real. What employees are experiencing emotionally outside the company's walls is not left behind as they arrive at work and swipe their ID badges. The sense of threat and insecurity is an underlying tension that saps productivity, and things only get worse when leaders don't acknowledge this reality. Our times call for leaders with the courage to speak about these polarizations and forge a third way. Omission through passivity is not a neutral stance. It can contribute to greater divisiveness.

Today's polarized environments can stir more blaming than bridge-building. Leaders can help all sides listen to one another, so they can acknowledge and own their parts in forging new solutions rather than merely blaming those with different points of view.

As I shared in my previous book, *Crisis as a Platform for Social Change from Strawberry Mansion to Silicon Valley*, so much of the 2016 presidential election was fueled by fear caused by economic dislocations for so many and exacerbated by scapegoating that has given way to ugly and frightening exhibits of hate. But most people are not haters. Yet most are scared and at a loss of what will restore their livelihoods, whether it's in the neglected inner cities or the neglected countryside. When leaders offer words of comfort and compassion, however, and encourage teams to take time out to talk about what is going on for each of them and to be heard by those who voted for a different candidate, it can help create integration among the societal, the personal, and the workplace.

Lead Authentically: Leaders should take this opportunity to demonstrate authentic leadership by making it personal, first through transparent reflection and then action. Leaders, like everyone else, are personally affected by these events. To be an effective leader in this context, it is helpful to pause and reflect on exactly what these effects are. This entails a process in which leaders connect with their core values, principles and beliefs. Authentic leadership begins with this kind of centering. Only by admitting to ourselves that we too are feeling vulnerable, afraid and even angry, and then doing the work of gathering perspective and strength from our core beliefs, can we then begin to offer genuine empathy and clearer thinking that will nurture more inclusive environments within our organizations.

From here, leaders can speak publicly and personally to create more relevance and connection. The most authentic stance from which to offer insight is from the vantage point of one's personal story. How did the 2016 presidential election affect each person emotionally and practically? Opinions can be debated as right or wrong, personal stories much less so.

Lead Boldly: Leaders should project a willingness to change. This one is offered by my colleague, Jim Rogers, author of numerous books on leadership, including *Managing Differently.*

Rogers suggests that anxious employees will look toward leaders who can adjust to change quickly. Inclusive leaders understand that they not only need to include others but must also include themselves as the first movers of change. It is paramount for leaders to change strategies, systems and cultures to transform organizations. But too often we forget the foundational, most elemental aspect of change: changing our own mind-set, heart-set and purpose-set. According to Rogers, CEOs who lead boldly accelerate positive, compelling, inclusive change. In times when strong, inclusive leadership is needed, corporate leaders should not forget to first be the change they want to see and then accelerate it.

Lead Confidently: On the protective side, of course, you want your organization to be vigilant about any hate speech and acts and be swift in addressing them. On the proactive side, with the three principles described here, get practical and act confidently by simply getting groups of employees talking. First, provide ground rules such as: Don't debate policies; instead, talk about needs and aspirations. Don't attack the person; discuss perspectives. Listen to understand rather than listen to debate.

And then go around and have each person in the conversation share what they hope to get out of life personally and for their family. Flipchart it, and once everyone has shared, start with the commonalities that emerged and slowly move into the differences. I suggest the group size be limited to ten to twelve people, and the group should have a skilled facilitator. Then replicate this throughout the organization.

The ideas here are modest compared to what will need to be done to address the high-stakes battles that will be fought in the public square with dramatic livelihood and even life-threatening implications for individuals, families and communities. But if we can simply get people who have become antagonistic, fearful and/or suspicious of one another due to their differences talking with each other, then each time we do, we can declare a small victory and build from there.

The Time for Argument Has Passed

The concept of civility, compassion and common decency that we expect from our coworkers is not being demonstrated by our civic leaders, and it's concerning to see how far that will go in the workplace. So, what can we realistically do about it? How can we reduce stress in the workplace and mitigate the emotional exhaustion felt by most of our employees?

In my book *Diversity Managers: Angels of Mercy or Barbarians at the Gate*, I suggest that "change starts with leadership." Leaders need to model positive behavior to help people work through their anxiety. This starts with acknowledging the unsettled feelings some people may be experiencing. Well over half (60 percent) of respondents to a 2017 Gallup survey said their companies hadn't communicated to their employees potential changes to health care, work visas or international travel. But staying silent or hoping that everyone works through it on their own is not an effective strategy.

Social crisis events like the travel ban require that we create a safe space to talk about social justice without inciting conflict by focusing on the feelings related to it, such as anxiety and uncertainty. This begins by gathering company leaders together to identify exactly what it is employees need to hear from the CEO and other senior leaders to settle their apprehension and anxiety. Focus on the things you can control, such as employees' workload, the tone and tenor of team discussions and how you react to the unexpected. Organizations should create a strategy and communication plan that acknowledges what people may be feeling and include consistent messaging across the entire organization.

Simple steps can make a big difference. Some best practices include organizations starting the workday with brief meditation exercises to help employees focus on the work at hand. Another popular best practice includes organizations insisting that employees step away from their desks intermittently for quick deep-breathing breaks or encouraging them to take a walk or refuel in the breakroom. The chief human resource officer at one company leads daily five-to-ten-minute dance breaks, inviting employees to participate in HR's version of the Soul Train Line or participating in line dances like The Wobble. Some other actions to consider:

- If your company offers EAP benefits, be sure that employees are aware of this and that they know how to access the confidential services.

- When necessary, call for a time-out on political discussion in the office. Such boundary-setting by managers can be a relief to team members who are still recovering from postelection stress and fatigue.
- Dial back the pressure on projects that don't demand it. Not everything is urgent. Revisit and reset, where appropriate, your team's priorities and communicate them clearly.
- If your workplace deals directly with customers, consider tuning TVs and radio stations in common areas to neutral stations such as cooking or home and garden programming. The same goes for TV monitors that may be in common areas shared by employees. One CHRO recently shared with me that at her company there was minor conflict over setting the channel to a specific cable news station. If you need to take a time-out and turn TV monitors off altogether, do it.

Implications for Diversity in America

The political climate since the 2016 presidential election has impacted the diversity and inclusion efforts in the workplace in one way or another. It does, and we all know it. From the rhetorical bombardment of the 2016 presidential election cycle to postinaugural developments, we are clearly distracted. Some of us may be anxious and worried; some of us may be annoyed by those who feel anxious and just wish everyone would take it easy and give things a chance to settle down.

I have been a human resource professional for over two decades. My specialty is diversity and inclusion — specifically, helping people around the corner and around the world to understand the inherent dignity of the individual and to manage organizations better by getting the best from all people. In my professional opinion, I believe it is time that diversity professionals help their organizations

77

transpose our efforts from simply increasing the number of women and people of color in organizations to focusing on healthy and inclusive behaviors. Inside the company, inclusive behaviors change how people treat each other. Beyond the company, they change how products can be designed, how to interact with the outside world and even the perspectives of suppliers, customers and communities.

Chapter 10 —
The Rise of Equity, Equality and Engagement

The conscience of America must be startled;
the hypocrisy of the country must be exposed.

Introduction

Following the presidential election of 2016, we are witnessing an impassioned debate playing out in our political and cultural worlds. Should we serve our own interests or the broader interests? Should we put America first or our own community? Should we place our company interests first, our customers' interests, or the environment? Should we place our career success as primary or our team's success? The answer to these and other salient questions is obvious. "Yes." We need to do it all.

The Power to Be Better

However, today's debate tries to force a decision — one or the other — on issues that call for dynamic and tough reconciliation. All our leadership research spanning millions of senior leaders globally suggests that leadership involves the constant reconciliation of the "I" and the "we" domains of leadership. When do we push and drive for our own way, excluding the views of others, and when do we involve others: listen, collaborate and synthesize their insights for a more diverse and inclusive view?

Since the presidential election of 2016, we see this debate play out across the country. On our teams, we are constantly deciding what to include and what to exclude. In our personal and family lives, as well, we attempt to be conscious of the "I" and "we," in terms of what drives our choices and the nature of our lives. It is not an easy task to find the sweet spot of the authentic, strong "I" and the connected, serving "we."

Since we opened our organizations and our lives as global citizens more than three decades ago, with the advent of the internet, exponential growth and the speed of new technologies, including access to abundant information and sci-fi-like connection, it would be like trying to put the digital genie back into the bottle to choose exclusion. With exclusion, we all lose. From a global business and human progress standpoint, is it really an option to choose exclusion over inclusion?

Moving from Organizational Comfort to Cultural Competence

In her book *Inclusion: Diversity in the Workplace and the Will to Change*, Jennifer Brown, an expert in workplace solutions and diversity and inclusion, makes a clear and critical distinction between diversity and inclusion for leaders. According to Brown, diversity is the mix and inclusion is making the mix work. Brown suggests that it is inclusion that is the crucial transformative challenge for twenty-first-century leaders. Brown makes a compelling case for inclusion as a business strategy, saying that if leaders want to attract and retain top talent, they must foster work environments in which they thrive.

I strongly agree with Jennifer Brown and believe that it is inclusion that unleashes talent and unpacks the power in teams making them more collaborative and creative. It is inclusion that optimizes and engages a multicultural work force and accelerates innovation. As a result, two things happen. First, employees become more engaged, collaborative, productive and innovative. Second, organizations expand existing markets, open new ones and develop new products based on a deeper understanding of customers, their cultures and unmet niches.

Brown suggests that inclusive leadership requires a deep understanding of how each of us is similar and dissimilar. Again, I agree with my good friend Jennifer Brown and would add that calling out differences unleashes the true creative contributions of diverse perspectives that play off each other and lead to better work relationships, greater innovation and profitability that benefits individuals, teams and organizations. Inclusive leaders leverage the differences on his or her team to make the team stronger. According to Jennifer Brown, we all have our unique differences. Every person has unique characteristics that define and influence the way he or she walks, talks, thinks, believes and acts the way he or she does.

Leaders must also become cross-culturally agile. At the heart of this cultural agility is emotional intelligence. This requires leaders to embrace and celebrate individual differences. Leaders need to understand in a deep, visceral, business-grounded way to activate diversity. Culturally incompetent managers seek control through uniformity. Authentic, culturally competent leaders create the future by being open and including the new, different and unusual.

Profiles in Cultural Competence and Courage

How does a person move from being an exclusive, culturally incompetent leader to be an inclusive, culturally competent leader? As I stated previously, it starts with emotional intelligence: seeing not only how and why we see the world the way we do but what we might be missing, our blind spots as individual leaders and as organ-

81

izations, and then finding seamless, relevant, applicable ways to embed cross-cultural agility in our daily lives and the work lives of time-constrained leaders.

Why don't more leaders and organizations make inclusion a priority? I believe it is because they don't know what they don't know. There is a gap in their authentic awareness. People think that diversity is enough, but to activate the promise of diversity, the creativity and innovation, leaders must become more than just open to others. They must become skilled and competent at inclusion. At the foundation of that competence is emotional intelligence.

An example of this is one of my clients, The Antares Group, is an example of a company working hard to embody diversity and inclusion. But it hasn't been easy. An embarrassing incident in which the company's president posted some unfavorable remarks on Twitter about NFL players kneeling during the national anthem provoked a backlash that caught the company off guard.

Instead of merely seeing this as a public relations incident requiring damage control, the president saw the experience as a wake-up call and a soul-searching journey of self-examination about who the company is and who the company thought it was. The incident provoked them to ask, "What else are we missing? What conscious or unconscious biases are holding us back from activating and achieving our goals?"

The company established an external Diversity Advisory Council of prominent community members and senior company leaders. The company also hired several consultants, including a minority-owned reputation management and multicultural marketing firm. The Diversity Advisory Council provided oversight of the work that included surveys, focus groups and leadership assessments. In addition, consultants interviewed all company leaders to assess their commitment to diversity and inclusion. Leaders and employees attended bias training with the goal of helping them integrate learning into their personal and daily work lives. The overall goal of their efforts was to become more diverse and lead more inclusively.

The company hired its first chief diversity officer (CDO), who, within months, made changes in internal policies that helped create a more inclusive work environment. For example, the CDO facilitated employee town halls that focused on issues of diversity and inclusion. In the months that followed, the company started to see a decrease in employee complaints about inappropriate remarks. Employees reported that they felt valued, respected and pride in the company's new direction and were glad to a part of it.

The company's intentional effort to include employees' unique perspectives sparked productivity and creativity, which eventually led to better product development, including a new software application customized for their client's toughest market.

The CEO has been a key leader in championing diversity and inclusion at the company, helping to implement its strategies and integrate it into daily operations. I interviewed the CEO, and he revealed that he intentionally looked for opportunities to spend time with employees who were different from him and discuss similarities and differences. In a moment of vulnerability, the CEO admitted that his personal goal was to move beyond tolerance to mutual respect. I asked him to provide a concrete example of what he had done to move from tolerance to a deeper level of respect. The CEO explained there was a time he would schedule a meeting on Good Friday, one of the holiest Christian days, and he would excuse the absence of Christian teammates: "that's tolerance." He explained that he no longer schedules meetings on Good Friday or other Christian holy days — "it's not much, but I'm trying to live and work with a deeper level of understanding and showing mutual respect."

83

Moving from Awareness to Action

After the economic recovery, several organizations experienced seismic change and reinvention, but they failed to keep pace with that growth by putting into place the internal policies and structures that would prevent disparate treatment toward certain employees — especially women. These failures stem from a toxic combination of ignorance on the part of senior leaders, the inability to see the impact of rapid growth and the internal dysfunction that ensued. In some cases, I believe the problem could also be attributed to intentional, company-level systemic bias.

So, what should companies be doing now? A good first step would be leadership holding themselves accountable to make their organizations truly modern workplaces that live up to egalitarian values. I recommend that CEOs and senior leaders listen to employees and train a new generation of managers and leaders in civility, compassion and common sense. In addition, the following actions have proven to be effective in organizations that have seen significant decreases in the number of sexual harassment complaints in their organizations.

- **Chief Compliance Officer:** Hire a chief compliance officer and give him or her broad authority to implement changes across the company.
- **Advisory Board:** Create an external Diversity and Inclusion Advisory Board chaired by a prominent "board-level" individual and empower this person to address critical issues of workplace culture and implement changes.
- **Pay Parity:** Commit to pay parity and hire an external consultant who is a leading expert on the issue.
- **Nontraditional Workplace Agreement:** Consult with the Diversity and Inclusion Advisory Board and develop a plan

to remove any "traditional" workplace agreements that employees were required to sign.

- **Maternity/Paternity Leave:** Expand maternity and paternity benefits for all full-time employees.

- **Policies, Procedures and Processes:** Clarify consensual relationships and sexual harassment policies and reporting procedures. Implement a confidential, third-party-operated, employee hotline to report issues or complaints.

- **Training Programs:** Revise compliance, diversity and inclusion training programs and enlist a well-known and experienced consultant with subject-matter expertise in organizational behavior and culture change. Ensure senior leaders complete the training first.

- **Chief Diversity Officer:** Expand the role of the chief diversity officer. Give the CDO the authority needed to improve efficiency and accountability in organizational culture and work environment.

- **Strategic Partners:** Sever ties with external organizations who espouse misogynistic and extremist ideologies.

Implications for Diversity in America

Following the presidential election of 2016, the truth is inescapable: from the top down, companies have failed as organizations to create safe and inclusive workplaces where everyone, especially women, feel valued and respected. I believe that cultural elements within most organizations, along with dysfunction and mismanagement, have allowed unhealthy behaviors to flourish unchecked. This includes a detrimental "boy's club" culture that has flourished for decades and inappropriate behavior that permeated throughout numerous organizations in the country.

It happened on our — diversity professionals' — watch, and ultimately, we let far too many people down. I believe I speak for most diversity professionals when I say that we understand that this had an impact on current and former employees at numerous organizations, and we regret our inability to prevent and extinguish discrimination, harassment, retaliation and other unhealthy — not to mention illegal — behaviors in our respective companies and society in general.

In recent months, we have seen numerous organizations take actions regarding multiple instances of unacceptable behavior. Several of these high-profile cases resulted in the termination of prominent corporate leaders. Unfortunately, there are still numerous organizations who are currently investigating allegations of sexual harassment that are being brought to their attention.

As a diversity professional, I had to answer a lot of questions from friends and colleagues after the 2016 presidential election. The question I was asked the most often was: "Are we safe?" Women asked me, "Are we safe?" LGBTQ people asked me, "Are we safe?" I never thought I would have to answer those questions because of the results of a presidential election. It's winter in America, and it seems everyone in the country needs some assurance of their safety and well-being. What we thought was initially presidential election campaign talk has continued after the election and now emboldens unhealthy behaviors.

We, diversity professionals, can no longer be a part of the problem — particularly if, as change agents, we want to investigate and address the many injustices in our companies, communities and the country. No matter your gender, race, ethnicity or sexual orientation, we need to do a better job at listening to and amplifying the stories and doubling down on our efforts to make our companies a place where all employees are valued, respected and productive.

In closing, I am reminded of a quote by Dr. Roosevelt Thomas, which summarizes the challenge in front of us: "Diversity is not casual, tolerance of anything and everything not yourself. Instead, diversity is — in action — the sometimes-painful awareness that other people, other races, other voices, other habits of minds, have as much integrity of being, as much claim on the world as you do. And I urge you, amid all the differences present to the eye and mind, to reach out to create the bond that will protect us all. We are meant to be here together."

Appendix A —
Suggested Additional Readings

Understanding the Link Between
Race and Community Cohesion

Bell, E. L. J., & Nkomo, S. M. (2001). *Our Separate Ways: Black and White Women and the Struggle for Professional Identity.* Boston: Harvard Business School Press.

Drawing on surveys of both black and white female managers, the authors show the profound impact of early life lessons on women's professional identities and reveal how geography and social location, when combined with race, play a powerful role in professional development.

Broadnax, W. D. (2000). *Diversity and Affirmative Action in Public Service.* Boulder, CO: Westview Press.

When it comes to creating a representative bureaucracy, *Diversity and Affirmative Action in Public Service* draws upon the most influential research and thought in public-administration literature to create a diverse public administrative work environment. Equal employment opportunity, gender and age discrimination and disability issues are also examined in detail.

Fernandez, J. P., & Davis, J. (1998). *Race, Gender and Rhetoric: The True State of Race and Gender Relations in Corporate America.* New York: McGraw-Hill.

Even though the authors admit that neither racism nor sexism can be fully eliminated, they insist each issue can be minimized by systematic and holistic strategies adopted to address broader human resource issues. The book argues that after thirty years of effort, corporate America has failed to effectively deal with such challenges posed by diversity. The authors outline six major steps that employees should embrace to enhance their career opportunities. This interesting book of theory and practice deserves widespread discussion.

Hopkins, W. E. (1997). *Ethical Dimensions of Diversity.* Thousand Oaks, CA: Sage.

This book takes an in-depth look at the relationship between the multiple dimensions of diversity and the ways diversity affects decision-making within organizations. The book uses a theoretical overview to identify points of potential conflict and subsequent effects on ethical paradigms. It also suggests ways of reconciling conflicts. *Ethical Dimensions of Diversity* gives diversity professionals the analytical skills and sensitivity necessary for dealing with difficult ethnicity and diversity issues.

Thomas, D. A., & Gabarro, J. J. (1999). *Breaking Through: The Making of Non-white Executives in Corporate America.* Boston: Harvard Business School Press.

Few nonwhite executives break through to the highest executive levels in corporate America, many times against odds. The aim of this book is to explain the processes of growth and advancement that produce nonwhite executives. *Breaking Through* examines both the individual and organizational factors influencing nonwhite promotion.

Thomas, R. R., Jr. (1992). *Beyond Race and Gender: Unleashing the Power of Your Total Workforce by Managing Diversity*. New York: AMACOM.

In the modern workforce, it is believed that only one in seven employees is a white male. The ability to manage such diversity successfully has now become a basic strategy for corporate survival. *Beyond Race and Gender* supplies an action plan, case studies and a series of tough questions and answers to provide readers with the ability to think deeply about elements that are blocking the full use of their employees.

Thomas, R. R., Jr., Thomas, D. A., Ely, R. J., & Meyerson, D. (2002). *Harvard Business Review on Managing Diversity*. Boston: Harvard Business School Publishing Corporation.

This book is a collection of classic and cutting-edge articles, case studies and first-person accounts of affirmative action. Additional topics on career development for nonwhites and women, as well as other human resource–related policies, are also included in this helpful book for managers.

Implementing a Strategic Diversity Management
Approach to Community Policing

Gardenswartz, L., & Rowe, A. (1998). *Managing Diversity: A Complete Desk Reference and Planning Guide* (Rev. Ed.). New York: McGraw-Hill.

Although many organizations understand the need for diversity awareness, many of them lack an effective organizational strategy. This book is packed with information, work sheets, charts and other valuable features for program implementation, as well as program evaluation and measurement. It also provides processes for conducting diversity audits and maximizing the talents of employees.

Gardenswartz, L., & Rowe, A. (1998). *Managing Diversity in Health Care: Proven Tools and Activities for Leaders and Trainers.* San Francisco: Jossey-Bass.

Sensitivity to and understanding of cultural diversity have become mandatory issues for professionals in health care. This is reflected in new cultural competency requirements for health care organizations. Most health care professionals have little or no training, however, when it comes to dealing with the challenges of cultural diversity. *Managing Diversity in Health Care* teaches effective strategies fundamental to creating a culturally diverse health care system.

Thomas, R. R., Jr. (1999). *Building a House for Diversity: A Fable About a Giraffe and Elephant Offers New Strategies for Today's Workforce.* New York: AMACOM.

91

Beginning with a short fable about how friendship between a giraffe and an elephant is threatened when the giraffe's house — built for tall, skinny giraffes — cannot accommodate his elephant friend, this story is a vivid metaphor for difficult issues inherent in diversity. *Building a House for Diversity* goes on to demonstrate how managing diversity is a set of useful skills that anyone can learn and use.

Thomas, R. R., Jr. (2006). *Building on the Promise of Diversity: How We Can Move to the Next Level in Our Workplaces, Our Communities, and Our Society*. New York: AMACOM.

Thomas believes most organizational leaders, as well as society, have come to accept a politicized definition of diversity, a definition that is now a code word for affirmative action. Such a definition positions diversity as a win/lose power struggle. It seems society views diversity through the lens of struggle because that is how society understands differences. This book clarifies the reader's understanding and thinking about diversity and show how to improve one's ability to manage diversity.

Advancing Gender Equality and Women's Diversity Initiatives

Hayles, R., & Russell, A. M. (1996). *The Diversity Directive: Why Some Initiatives Fail and What to Do About It*. New York: McGraw-Hill.

Organizations across the nation have implemented diversity programs designed to produce multicultural corporate environments. *The Diversity Directive* helps readers guide their organizations through the process of planning and implementing a diversity program that sustains real and lasting cultural change, as well as realizes the rewards of their efforts.

Kiselica, M. S. (1998). *Confronting Prejudice and Racism During Multicultural Training.* Alexandria, VA: American Counseling Association.

Confronting Prejudice and Racism During Multicultural Training examines multicultural-training program components to assess how trainees adopt, digest or resist multicultural principles and practices. There are two parts to this book. The first part, "Theoretical and Practical Considerations," speaks of theory as well as issues of putting theory into practice. The second section, "Recommendations for Multicultural Educators," discusses recommendations for multicultural training.

Lasch-Quinn, E. (2001). *Race Experts: How Racial Etiquette, Sensitivity Training, and New Age Therapy Hijacked the Civil Rights Revolution.* New York: W. W. Norton & Company.

Probing the intersection of the civil rights struggle and modern social psychology, Lasch-Quinn highlights the overthrow of the social code of segregation and the adoption of etiquette of black assertiveness and white submissiveness. Such an adoption of etiquette has produced a *harangue-flagellation* ritual that does not advance the goal of racial equality, according to the author. It seems such etiquette will make interaction between the races a social minefield, discouraging contact. Lasch-Quinn also discusses how cottage industries have perpetuated differentiation among the races.

Loden, M. (1995). *Implementing Diversity: Best Practices for Making Diversity Work in Your Organization.* New York: McGraw-Hill.

A practical and provocative guide that provides strategies and tactics used by organizations committed to implementing diversity and inclusion within their organization. This book focuses on the necessity for strategic-change initiatives when it comes to diversity and inclusion. *Implementing Diversity* discusses how to position diversity-management initiatives for maximum support, proven strategies for managing resistance and the classic mistakes made when implementing diversity-management initiatives and how to avoid them.

Martin, J. (2001). *Profiting from Multiple Intelligences in the Workplace*. Burlington, VT: Gower Publishing Company.

Economic competitiveness depends on having the most intelligent workforce possible. Organizations that want to survive and prosper need to be open to new ways of uncovering and developing their employees' abilities. *Profiting from Multiple Intelligences in the Workplace*, Martin's revolutionary theory of multiple intelligences introduces user-friendly tools for understanding and assessing employees' skills and abilities. As a result, organizations will have the necessary tools to uncover the mosaic of abilities needed for multi-skills, multitasking, and efficient teamwork.

Orey, M. C. (1996). *Successful Staffing in a Diverse Workplace: A Practical Guide to Building an Effective and Diverse Staff*. Irvine, CA: Richard Chang Associates.

From recruiting to orientation, the way an organization staffs its workforce determines how such a workforce performs as a team. This guidebook shows how managers can successfully deal with each element involved in staffing a diverse workforce.

Examining Gridlock in Race Relations in America

Marsden, D. (1999). *A Theory of Employment Systems: Micro foundations of Societal Diversity.* New York: Oxford University Press.

This book discusses why there are great international differences in the way employment relations are organized within organizations. Taking account of the growing evidence that international diversity is not being eradicated by globalization, it begins with the theory of the organization and explains why organizations and workers need to use the employment relationship as a basis for economic cooperation.

Shelton, J. S. (1994). *The Future of White Men and Other Diversity Dilemmas.* Berkeley, CA: Conari Press.

The author suggests ways to handle oneself in culturally sensitive situations. As a spokesperson and news-column writer on diversity issues, Shelton expresses thoughts that are straightforward and easily understood, such as being sensitive to others' backgrounds, including ethnicity, gender, and age. Destruction of stereotypes and ethnic humor are also discussed.

Examining the Link Between Diversity Management and Religious Practices Organizations

Albrecht, M. H. (2000). *International HRM: Managing Diversity in the Workplace.* Malden, MA: Blackwell Business.

This collection of articles and case studies helps readers develop the knowledge, skills and attitudes managers need for success when working in culturally diverse environments. Three key questions are addressed within the book: (1) What are the trends and current issues in global diversity that affect management and human resources? (2) What are the solutions? (3) What is needed to implement these solutions? This step-by-step book provides diversity managers with the skills necessary to become culturally competent practitioners. The book's process draws on the author's twenty years of cultural-diversity work, as well as the fundamental premise that cultural competence is an ongoing, multilayered process that involves personal, interpersonal, and organizational levels. Divided into four skills, including cultural awareness, understanding, interpersonal techniques and organizational change, each chapter combines cognitive and experiential learning.

Cox, T., Jr. (2001). *Creating the Multicultural Organization: A Strategy for Capturing the Power of Diversity* (1st Ed.). San Francisco: Jossey-Bass.

Organizations are seeking proven methods for leveraging workforce diversity as a resource, especially as the war for talent rages on. *Creating the Multicultural Organization* challenges organizations to stop counting their diverse workforce for the government and begin creating effective strategies that will create a positive approach for managing diversity. This book utilizes a model outlined in Cox's previous work and shows readers the many practical and innovative ways that successful organizations address diversity issues to secure and develop talent within their workforce to succeed.

Thiederman, S. (1995). *Getting Culture Smart: Ten Strategies for Making Diversity Work*. Broomfield, CO: Cross-Cultural Communications.

This book is applicable to all types of diversity. It is perfect for anyone who works or lives around diverse people. Designed as a desk reference tool, *Getting Culture Smart* is ideal for those who need to know about diversity but lack the time to do in-depth reading. *Getting Culture Smart* discusses ten strategies for dealing with diversity, such as finding commonalities among people, diffusing stereotypical thinking and developing skills for communicating respect.

Thiederman, S. (2003). *Making Diversity Work: Seven Steps for Defeating Bias in the Workplace*. Chicago: Dearborn Trade Publishing.

Bias lies in every heart and mind, according to Thiederman. The heart and mind are also where the answer lies to defeating bias. By focusing on individual rather than organizational processes, powerful focus for bias-busting can be obtained within the workplace. Utilizing case studies, politically incorrect questions and insightful strategies, Thiederman guides readers through the discomfort of self-discovery.

Evaluating the Link Between Societal Challenges on Corporate Culture

Arredondo, P. M. (1996). *Successful Diversity Management Initiatives: A Blueprint for Planning and Implementation*. Thousand Oaks, CA: Sage.

Outlining specific steps for a diversity-management process, Arredondo brings a fresh, insightful and helpful blueprint for beginning, as well as advancing, diversity-management initiatives. The book discusses the rationale for procedures, identifies potential roadblocks and explores how barriers can be managed. Specific examples based on the author's research and experiences with organizations are given to help readers obtain an integrative and systematic perspective about issues involved in diversity and inclusion.

Chang, R. Y. (1999). *Capitalizing on Workplace Diversity*. San Francisco: Jossey-Bass-Pfeiffer.

Few issues present such a unique combination of challenges and potential benefits in the workplace as that of diversity. *Capitalizing on Workplace Diversity* is a guidebook that goes beyond handling the challenges of diversity and focuses on how diversity can be tapped as core strength to an organization. This book provides managers with a practical guide on creating a diversity vision, building commitment, ensuring worker capability and reinforcing success.

Cox, T., Jr., & Beale, R. L. (1997). *Developing Competency to Manage Diversity: Reading, Cases, and Activities* (1st Ed.). San Francisco: Berrett-Koehler Publishers.

The ability to successfully manage diversity is a major initiative for many organizations. *Developing Competency to Manage Diversity* organizes learning and skill-building for diversity and inclusion around activities that can change behavior, address a wide variety of diversity issues, integrate ideas from academia with real-life experiences and provide managers with tools they need to manage a diverse workforce successfully.

Cross, E. Y., & White, M. B. (Eds.). (1996). *The Diversity Factor: Capturing the Competitive Advantage of a Changing Workforce*. Chicago: Irwin Professional Pub.

With the changing face of America, the workforce of the twenty-first century will include a growing number of women and people of color. Organizations must develop new management skills if they want to remain competitive in this new environment. This book compiles the most requested articles from *The Diversity Factor*, a quarterly journal, and provides both theoretical and practical information that will help organizations learn to manage diversity successfully.

DeLong, D. W. (2004). *Lost Knowledge: Confronting the Threat of an Aging Workforce.* Oxford University Press.

This book shows how losing human knowledge in a technology intensive era can seriously affect organizational performance. It also explains what executives can do to retain critical knowledge as veteran workers leave. The author has loaded the book with anecdotes and case examples and reveals how this hidden problem, which threatens virtually all industrialized nations, is becoming extremely serious for many organizations.

DiversityInc. (2006). *The Business Case for Diversity* (5th Ed.). Newark, NJ: DiversityInc.

Workplace and marketplace diversity are marks of a well-managed company. This book illustrates how creating an inclusive culture benefits the bottom line. This is a must-read for diversity leaders, as this book includes advice and examples from top-performing companies, evidence of how diversity increases retention, information about the cornerstones of successful diversity-management initiatives and much more important and relevant information.

Esty, K., & Griffin, R. (1995). *Workplace Diversity: A Manager's Guide to Solving Problems and Turning Diversity into a Competitive Advantage*. Avon, MA: Adams Media.

This book assists managers of diverse workforces in solving problems and turning a diverse work environment into a competitive advantage rather than a liability.

Flood, R. L., & Romm, N. R. A. (1996). *Diversity Management: Triple Loop Learning*. New York: J. Wiley.

Diversity Management provides a strong intellectual contribution to the widely debated issue of diversity and inclusion. It carefully blends theory and practice to provide substance to the debate on managing diversity in the social and systems sciences. It is thoughtfully illustrated with case studies and brings an overall awareness to the process of diversity and inclusion, so it is more reflexive and those involved can operate more intelligently and responsibly.

Gentile, M. C. (1996). *Managerial Excellence Through Diversity Cases*. Chicago: Irwin.

Gentile explains that diversity is not a problem to be managed away. It is, however, an opportunity to develop greater personal and organizational performance. This book includes all dimensions of diversity in the workforce and customer base, including race, gender, ethnicity and nationality, just to name a few, and teaches professionals how to respond effectively to the increasingly diverse business environment.

Hanamura, S. (2005). *I Can See Clearly*. New York: Renaissance Publishers.

Intended to show leaders and decision-makers new possibilities for leading a diverse workforce, *I Can See Clearly* uses the power of personal stories as the catalyst to introduce creative thinking on how to address workplace challenges and ensure that all members of society have become contributing members of the workforce.

Pearn, M. (Ed.). (2002). *Individual Differences and Development in Organizations*. West Sussex, England: John Wiley & Sons, Ltd.

This handbook provides a unique and authoritative review of relevant research, theoretical developments and current best practices in the management of individual development. This book is designed to be a practical guide and support for those whose role it is to bring out the development of people in the workforce.

Measuring the Impact of Diversity Management on Corporate and Community Relations

Hubbard, E. E. (1997). *Measuring Diversity Results*. Petaluma, CA: Global Insights Pub.

Measuring Diversity Results provides formulas for measuring results. It is beneficial to organizations that promote only those individuals who fall into a certain mold. By determining results, changes can be made that are beneficial to the entire workforce, not just a chosen few.

Hubbard, E. E. (1999). *How to Calculate Diversity Return on Investment.* Petaluma, CA: Global Insights Pub.

The approach found in this book helps diversity managers calculate their organizations' return on investment, reduce the cycle time to create diversity measures, link diversity efforts to organizational goals, provide a way to combine diversity and organizational measures and provide options for valuing the process given the type of organizational work or process being measured.

Hubbard, E. E. (2003). *The Manager's Pocket Guide to Diversity Management.* Amherst, MA: HRD Press.

This pocket guide provides managers with the skills required to effectively manage a diverse workforce. It helps diversity professionals gain awareness, tools, knowledge and techniques necessary to raise morale, improve processes and enhance productivity while improving the bottom line. *The Manager's Pocket Guide to Diversity Management* contains workplace applications for weaving diversity into recruitment and selection, employee retention and development and team-building. This pocket guide is an invaluable tool for managers and leaders.

Hubbard, E. E. (2005). *The Diversity Scorecard: Evaluating the Impact of Diversity on Organizational Effectiveness.* Burlington, MA: Elsevier Butterworth-Heinemann.

The Diversity Scorecard does not focus on just one sector of diversity and inclusion. It provides strategies, tactics and communication approaches for all types of organizations. It takes readers from theory to practice and shows how professionals can develop their own diversity and inclusion scorecard from beginning to end.

Understanding the Four Generations
in the Workplace and Marketplace

Cobbs, P. M., & Turnock, J. L. (2003). *Cracking the Corporate Code: The Revealing Success Stories of 32 African-American Executives*. New York: AMACOM.

The authors of this book surveyed more than thirty influential African American executives to discuss their strategies for dealing with racial, cultural and organizational challenges. The content combines strong narrative and stirring quotes and tackles several issues, including race and gender bias, isolation and competition and diversity. *Cracking the Corporate Code* provides inspirational guidance for young African Americans considering a corporate career.

Cross, E. Y. (2000). *Managing Diversity: The Courage to Lead*. Westport, CT: Quorum Books.

Drawing on her African American background, Cross provides the practical assistance today's organizational leaders need. She demonstrates how oppression functions at individual, group and system levels. She makes clear that if executives are to solve such problems, they must confront their own emotional and psychological barriers. This knowledgeable book is a major contribution to the understanding of gender and cultural problems, as well as a sign of hope that both can be solved.

Iwata, K. (2004). *The Power of Diversity: 5 Essential Competencies for Leading a Diverse Workforce*. Petaluma, CA: Global Insights.

Offering specific guidelines and tools to increase competency at managing and leading a diverse workforce, *The Power of Diversity* draws from a field study of sixteen companies. This book allows the reader to assess his or her level of diversity competence, while activities provide an opportunity to sharpen skills and abilities.

Lieberman, S., Simons G., & Berardo, K. (2003). *Putting Diversity to Work: How to Successfully Lead a Diverse Workforce*. Toronto, Canada: Crisp Publications, Inc.

Employing people from different backgrounds can give organizations an edge, both internally and externally. This book helps managers integrate diversity and inclusion into their search for highly skilled, multitalented employees. It shows how to recruit the best people and build a creative, flexible, inclusive workforce. Additionally, effective communication skills, rapport-building and management conflict resolution are included in this book on diversity.

Sonnenschein, W. (1997). *The Practical Executive and Workforce Diversity*. New York: McGraw-Hill.

The Practical Executive and Workforce Diversity helps every manager translate the potential benefits of modern diverse workforces into tangible, productive workplace gains. This book contains practical guidance for improving team-building relationships and more.

Srivastva, S., & Cooperrider, D. L. (1999). *Appreciative Management and Leadership: The Power of Positive Thought and Action in Organization*. Brunswick, OH: Crown Custom Publishing.

Organizations in the twenty-first century look very different from those in the past. Faced with an environment of unpredictable demands and a workforce of great cultural and ethnic diversity, organizations will have to find new ways of engaging their members in a spirit of common purpose. This book offers a new perspective on management that allows executives to unlock their organizations' potential for creativity, innovation and collaboration.

Gauging the Degrees of Separation
Between the Five Generations

Deresky, H. (1999). *International Management: Managing Across Borders and Cultures* (3rd Ed.). Upper Saddle River, NJ: Prentice Hall.

This book covers the most current research and trends in international management. It offers comprehensive and integrative cases illustrating actual behaviors and functions that are required for successful cross-cultural management at both the strategic and interpersonal levels. *International Management* is a great resource for international business professionals.

Dowling, P. J., Welch, D. E., & Schuler, R. S. (1999). *International Human Resource Management: Managing People in a Multinational Context*. Cincinnati, OH: South Western College Publishing.

While covering key topics on international human resource management, this book also refers to the emerging theory and issues related to such management.

Elliott, C. (1999). *Locating the Energy for Change: An Introduction to Appreciative Inquiry.* New York: International Institute for Sustainable Development.

The main purpose of this book is for readers to understand what appreciative inquiry is and how it can be utilized to change organizations. Elliott speaks of how feeling is just as important as understanding and that appreciative inquiry takes the energy from the positive present and uses it to build a vision of a positive, desired future that is grounded.

Gardenswartz, L., Rowe, A., Digh, P., & Bennett, M. F. (2003). *The Global Diversity Desk Reference: Managing an International Workforce.* San Francisco: Pfeiffer.

This book provides readers with conceptual models, practical guides and training tools to lead, manage, facilitate and coach a diverse workforce. It equips intellectuals to reach higher creativity and performance in global business. This is a highly recommended book for professionals in global diversity.

Granrose, C. S., & Oskamp, S. (1997). *Cross-Cultural Work Groups.* Thousand Oaks, CA: Sage Publications.

This book pulls together findings from several disciplines and presents the most current research available on cross-cultural work groups. It explores issues that are often present when different cultural groups are brought together, as well as issues of prejudice, discrimination, ethnocentrism and intergroup dynamics.

Harris, P. R., Moran, R. T., & Moran, S. V. (2004). *Managing Cultural Differences: Global Leadership Strategies for the 21st Century.* Burlington, MA: Elsevier Butterworth-Heinemann.

The authors of *Managing Cultural Differences* have constructed a valuable network of resources for multicultural managers. They provide new pathways to competence on a global scale grounded in empirical research and illustrated by fascinating stories and examples. Guiding readers toward an accurate awareness of their own cultural identity relative to others, the authors provide meaningful knowledge about the facts and information necessary to comprehend cultural context and take appropriate action in making decisions that benefit all parties.

Morosini, P. (1998). *Managing Cultural Differences: Effective Strategy and Execution Across Cultures in Global Corporate Alliances.* New York: Pergamon.

Managing Cultural Differences examines the complexities of cultural and organizational differences that arise during mergers and acquisitions, joint ventures and alliances. According to the book, more than 50 percent of all corporate alliances fail, and those across cultural divides are even less likely to succeed. Such failures can be attributed to executives concentrating on the financial aspects of a deal rather than, and at the expense of, cultural, organizational and execution aspects.

Tayeb, M. H. (1996). *Management of a Multicultural Workforce*. New York: Wiley.

The existence of a multicultural workforce has important implications for human resource management policies. This book takes a systematic approach to relating organizational features and activities to specific national cultures. This book will be of interest to managers, as well as researchers and MBA students.

Leveraging Employee Resource Groups, Diversity Councils and High-Performance Teams to Enhance Organizational Performance

Gardenswartz, L., & Rowe, A. (1995). *Diverse Teams at Work: Capitalizing on the Power of Diversity*. Chicago: Irwin Professional Pub.

Making differences in the workplace an asset rather than a liability can be accomplished through strategies provided in *Diverse Teams at Work*. This practical guide gives team members ways to understand and make the most of their differences while overcoming barriers to achievement—barriers that are often the result of diversity. The book also provides worksheets, processes, guidance and tools to learn how to diversify groups while building relationships. An annotated list of resources is also provided.

Goode, S. J. (2014). *Diversity Managers: Angels of Mercy or Barbarians at the Gate*. Indianapolis: iUniverse Publishing.

Why do some diversity strategies contribute to organizational success while other strategies fail to launch? The answer, according to the author, is that successful diversity managers can implement diversity initiatives that produce results.

Diversity Managers: Angels of Mercy or Barbarians at the Gate is valuable for a wide audience because it provides diversity practitioners and business leaders alike with a diversity GPS that helps them pinpoint areas that may be strengths and opportunities in their organizations.

This book is based on extensive research and practical experience. Goode challenges diversity efforts that are based on untested assumptions and provides diversity practitioners with battle-tested strategies that enhance organizational performance. *Diversity Managers: Angels of Mercy or Barbarians at the Gate* empowers diversity managers by providing them with knowledge and insights to advance their organizations' diversity and inclusion strategies.

Jackson, S. E., & Ruderman, M. N. (1995). *Diversity in Work Teams: Research Paradigms for a Changing Workplace* (5th Ed.). Washington, DC: American Psychological Association.

This book explores how diversity affects one of the most popular management strategies employed by business leaders today. That popular strategy is the formation of employee work teams. Organizations must learn to understand and adjust to workplace diversity, as many of the specific assets and liabilities of work teams arise directly from the diverse talents and perspectives inherent in them.

Karp, H. (2002). *Bridging the Boomer-Xer Gap: Creating Authentic Teams for High Performance at Work*. Mountain View, CA: Davies-Black Publishing.

It seems the stereotypical notion that Generation Xers are more individualistic than baby boomers is not true, at least in the research conducted by Karp. In fact, Generation Xers are real team players, perhaps even more so than boomers. There are only subtle differences that separate the boomers and Xers when it comes to working on teams. This book is recommended for those who are pursuing solid, general team-management guidance, as well to manage cross-generational workers.

Considering Diversity Management as a Force of Societal and Cultural Change

Goode, S. J. (2016). *Crisis as a Platform for Social Change from Strawberry Mansion to Silicon Valley.* Denver, CO: Outskirts Press.

Crisis as a Platform For Social Change from Strawberry Mansion to Silicon Valley is Goode's impassioned wakeup call to take our understanding of diversity to a wholly new level — beyond finger pointing and well-meaning initiatives and toward the shared goal of building inclusive communities, robust companies and a thriving county. This original and thought-provoking book helps leaders in any setting — business, educational, religious, educational, community — break out of the status quo and reinvigorate the spirit "that we can do better than this."

The book, which charts Goode's own evolution in diversity thinking, includes deeply felt personal perspectives on tensions and uncertainties that result from society awakening to the fact that it is becoming more diverse and struggling with the social and political changes to make it more inclusive.

Kossek, E. E., & Lobel, S. A. (1996). *Managing Diversity: Human Resource Strategies for Transforming the Workplace.* Cambridge, MA: Blackwell Business.

This book considers the implications of workforce diversity for the development and synthesis of specific human resource policies.

Contributors provide a range of perspectives on significance of workforce diversity as it relates to human resources, as well as the workplace in general. Additionally, the degrees to which current theory and practice have incorporated issues of diversity and inclusion are discussed.

Leach, J. G., Bette, J., & Labelle, A. (1995). *A Practical Guide to Working with Diversity: The Process, the Tools, and the Resources.* New York: AMACOM.

There has been much inspirational talk about diversity and the importance of managing it properly. Working with differences and not against them is very important when dealing with diversity issues. This book is a pragmatic guide that gives readers everything they need to know to implement an effective diversity and inclusion plan within their organization.

Lebo, F. (1996). *Mastering the Diversity Challenge: Easy On-the-Job Applications for Measurable Results.* Delray Beach, FL: St. Lucie Press.

Mastering the Diversity Challenge is an easy-to-use guidebook that goes beyond the basic requirements for mastering diversity. It gives important reasons on why managing diversity is good for overall business success.

Wilson, T. (1998). *Diversity at Work: The Business Case for Equity*. Ontario, Canada: John Wiley & Sons.

Diversity at Work is a hands-on, practical guide to the why and how to strive for diversity and equality in the workplace. It guides managers in creating a fair employment system for all employees, accommodating and valuing differences, hiring and retaining the best-qualified people for jobs and overcoming backlash associated with controversial affirmative action and employment legislation, plus many more issues. It is a must-have for managing professionals.

Creating Inclusive Places to Work, Live and Play

Brown, J. (2017). *Inclusion: Diversity, the Workplace & the Will to Change*. Hartford, CT: Publish Your Purpose Press.

In the rapidly changing business landscape, harnessing the power of diversity and inclusion is essential for the very viability and sustainability of every organization. Talent who feel fully welcomed, valued, respected and heard by their colleagues and their organizations will fuel this growth. We will only succeed in this transformation if those in leadership pivot from command and control management styles to reinvent how we look at people, every organization's greatest asset. It's also critical that we build systems that embrace diversity in all its forms, from identity and background to diversity of thought, style, approach and experience, tying it directly to the bottom line. *Inclusion: Diversity, the New Workplace & the Will to Change* stands up for and embraces what true diversity and inclusion represent to any organization in any industry: an opportunity. Open your heart and prepare to be inspired as award-winning entrepreneur, dynamic speaker and respected diversity and inclusion expert Brown shares proven strategies to empower members of your entire organization to utilize all their talents and potential to drive positive organizational change and the future of work.

Bucher, R., & Bucher, P. (2003). *Diversity Consciousness: Opening Our Minds to People, Cultures, and Opportunities.* New York: Prentice Hall.

The ability to understand, respect and value diversity is an empowering personal attribute. This book demonstrates how opening one's mind to the views of other peoples and cultures is central to quality education and a successful career. *Diversity Consciousness* provides a variety of real-life experiences and perspectives throughout the book. It discusses topics in a style that promotes self-reflection and dialogue while using an approach to diversity that is balanced, comprehensive, well-integrated and relevant to achieving one's life goals.

Chemers, M., Oskamp, S., & Constanzo, M. (Ed.). (1995). *Diversity in Organizations: New Perspectives for a Changing Workplace.* Thousand Oaks, CA: Sage Publications, Inc.

The largest percentage of new workers in the coming decades will be those considered nontraditional employees. Such new workforce diversity presents both challenges and opportunities to individuals and organizations alike. Benefits include a broader talent pool and development of potential. However, new perspectives can create tension, misunderstanding and even hostility. *Diversity in Organi-*

113

zations helps readers come to grips with new diversity issues by applying varied perspectives and approaches in a scholarly manner that is both contemporary and insightful.

Cobbs, P. M., & Turnock, J. L. (2000). *Cracking the Corporate Code: From Survival to Mastery.* Washington, DC: Executive Leadership Council.

Although written from a uniquely African American perspective, this book speaks to the human experience, making it relevant for anyone seeking advice and inspiration to succeed in a diverse workforce. It offers informative and inspirational self-help career development via the career stories and success strategies of thirty-two senior-level African American executives in Fortune 500 companies.

Hanamura, S. (2000). *In Search of Vision: Finding Significance Through Difference.* Petaluma, CA: Global Insights.

This thought-provoking, motivational and inspirational book integrates Hanamura's life experiences into applications from both home and business. It weaves together all aspects of his life as a single parent, a Christian, a blind person, a child of a blended family and a corporate consultant to teach breakthrough concepts about the process of living and working together. He demonstrates how his own life has been affected through understanding the importance of humility and surrendering his life to accomplish a purpose God has intended for him.

Harvey, C., & Allard, M. J. (2002). *Understanding and Managing Diversity: Readings, Cases, and Exercises.* Upper Saddle River, NJ: Prentice Hall.

This book provides cases and exercises organized in terms of three perspectives: individual, social-group identity and organizational diversity. It also includes classic diversity and inclusion contributions by well-known authors such as Peggy McIntosh, Milton Bennett, David Thomas and more. Difficult-to-find original teaching material topics such as the business case for diversity, ethics and board diversity are also included in this edition. Coverage of multiple aspects of workforce diversity beyond race, gender and ethnicity are also discussed, along with features such as assessment assignments and web-based exercises.

Lecca, P. J. (1998). *Cultural Competency in Health, Social & Human Services: Directions for the 21st Century.* Dallas: Garland.

As thousands of people come to the United States each year, cultural competency is an issue that is becoming increasingly more important. Health care professionals are finding it difficult to communicate effectively with the members of diverse racial and ethnic backgrounds who come to them for help. This book presents the latest information and techniques for improving cultural competency in health, social and human services to those individuals of ethnic and racial minorities. Anyone who meets ethnic and racial minorities will benefit from such information and techniques.

Norton, J. R., & Fox, R. E. (1997). *Change Equation: Capitalizing on Diversity for Effective Organizational Change.* Washington, DC: American Psychological Association.

Showing how to tap into the power of existing diversity within an organization, this book demonstrates how managers can turn such diverse environments into pluralistic workplaces where change is something to embrace, not something to resist. Organizational change agents, business leaders, human resource managers and anyone wanting to make his or her organization stronger and more competitive will find in this book a wealth of practical solutions to advance their organizations.

Prasad, P. M., Albert, J., Elmes, M., & Prasad, A. (1997). *Managing the Organizational Melting Pot: Dilemmas of Workplace Diversity.* Thousand Oaks, CA: Sage Publications, Inc.

Managing the Organizational Melting Pot covers key issues related to diversity, such as individual and institutional resistance, performance of diversity-change efforts and exclusion and discrimination issues — issues that most management literature glosses over. The contributors to this collection adopt an array of theoretical frameworks to assist readers in understanding some of diversity's dilemmas. A departure from the more traditional and functional perspective on diversity, this book employs a variety of theoretical perspectives, such as intergroup-relations theory, critical theory and postmodernism, just to name a few. All in all, this book is beneficial to managers as well as researchers dealing with issues of diversity.

Rodgers, J. O., & Hunter, M. (2004). *Managing Differently: Getting 100% from 100% of Your People 100% of the Time.* Winchester, VA: Oakhill Press.

This handbook for leaders is a great tool in the ever-changing diverse workplace. *Managing Differently* begins with the notion that diversity and inclusion initiatives should focus on managers and their leadership capabilities. This practical approach makes it possible to improve communications in an organization as well as improve performance. Everyone in an organization wants to feel valued, and it is the manager's responsibility to create an environment where everyone feels valued and employee engagement is natural.

Sonnenschein, W. (1999). *The Diversity Toolkit: How You Can Build and Benefit from a Diverse Workforce.* Lincolnwood, IL: Contemporary Books.

With help from this book, managers of all levels can learn to adapt and be sensitive to new workforce realities. *The Diversity Toolkit* features easy-to-use tips for improving communication skills, practical guidance for perfecting team relationships and helpful suggestions for using disability metaphors to teach leadership principles that supplement best practices in business as well as in transformational thinking, and ideas and strategies for creating a positive workplace environment.

Defining Diversity and Other Terms Used in the Field of Diversity Management

Pringle, J., Konrad, A. M., & Prasad, P. (2006). *Handbook of Workplace Diversity.* Thousand Oaks, CA: Sage.

By assembling an international cast of contributors from all walks of research life, Prasad, Pringle and Konrad successfully broaden the scope of scholarly discourse on workplace diversity. This stimulating volume considers how to define this fuzzy construct, what differences are more important than others and how to make best

117

use of alternative research methods at different levels of analysis. It reviews what we have learned about workplace diversity along several important dimensions (e.g., gender, race, ethnicity, weight, sexual orientation, disabilities, class), and it offers useful recommendations for how to conduct future research that will expand our knowledge of the implications of diversity for individuals, marginalized groups, work organizations and societies.

In this much-needed handbook, an international collection of first-rate scholars deals incisively and perceptively with the problems of diversity, difference, inclusion and cultural pluralism in organizations. This handbook will be invaluable for researchers and advanced students — one of those books that stays on the top of the desk, covered with bookmarks. Globalization and its melting pot of different nationalities, ethnicities and cultures is attracting research that is gathering in substance and theory. A dynamic new field that represents a significant focus within management and organization studies is emerging.

This handbook showcases the scope of international perspectives that exists on workplace diversity and is the first to define this hotly contested field.

Appendix B —
Selected Terms and Definitions

ableism — Discrimination against persons with mental and/or physical disabilities; social structures that favor able-bodied individuals (The National Multicultural Institute).

acculturation — The process of addressing cultural differences, cultural change and adaptation between groups. Acculturation is the process of learning and incorporating the language, values, beliefs and behaviors that make up a distinct culture. This concept is not to be confused with assimilation, where an individual or group may give up certain aspects of their culture to adapt to that of the prevailing culture (The National Multicultural Institute).

affirmative action — Proactive policies and procedures for remedying the effect of past discrimination and ensuring the implementation of equal employment and educational opportunities, for recruiting, hiring, training and promoting women, minorities, people with disabilities and veterans in compliance with the federal requirements enforced by the Office of Federal Contract Compliance Programs (OFCCP). Affirmative action includes specific actions in recruiting, hiring and promoting to eliminate the present effects of past discrimination, or to prevent discrimination (Society for Human Resources Management).

affirmative action plan — The written document through which management ensures that all persons have equal opportunities in recruitment, selection, appointment, promotion, training, discipline and related employment areas. The plan is tailored to the employer's workforce and the skills available in the labor force. It prescribes specific actions, goals, timetables and responsibilities, and describes resources to meet identified needs. The plan is a comprehensive, results-oriented program designed to achieve equal employment opportunity rather than merely to ensure nondiscrimination (The National Multicultural Institute).

ageism — Discrimination against individuals because of their age, often based on stereotypes (The National Multicultural Institute).

ally — A person who acts against oppression out of a belief that eliminating oppression will benefit members of targeted groups and advantage groups. Allies acknowledge disadvantage and oppression of groups other than their own, take supportive action on their behalf, commit to reducing their own complicity or collusion in oppression of these groups and invest in strengthening their own knowledge and awareness of oppression (Center for Assessment and Policy Development).

American Indian (Native American) or Alaska Native — A person having origin in any of the original peoples of North America and who maintains cultural identification through tribal affiliation or community recognition (The National Multicultural Institute).

anti-oppression — Recognizing and deconstructing the systemic, institutional and personal forms of disempowerment used by certain groups over others; actively challenging the different forms of oppression (Center for Anti-Oppressive Education).

Asian or Pacific Islander — A person having origin in any of the original peoples of the Far East, Southeast Asia, the Indian Subcontinent or the Pacific Islands. This area includes China, Japan, Korea, the Philippine Islands and Samoa.

120

bias — A subjective opinion, preference or prejudice without reasonable justification that is detrimental to a group's or an individual's ability to treat ideas or people objectively. Bias is a positive or negative inclination toward a person, group or community; can lead to stereotyping

bigot — An obstinate and intolerant believer in a religion, political theory and so on (The National Multicultural Institute).

bigotry — Intolerant prejudice that glorifies one's own group and denigrates members of other groups (Dismantling Racism Institute).

bisexuality — Romantic and/or sexual attraction to people of more than one sex and/or gender, not necessarily at the same time, not necessarily in the same way and not necessarily to the same degree (Ochs).

bullying — Intimidating, exclusionary, threatening or hostile behavior against an individual.

Chicano/a — A term adopted by some Mexican Americans to demonstrate pride in their heritage, born out of the national Chicano Movement that was politically aligned with the civil rights movement to end racial oppression and social inequalities of Mexican Americans. Chicano pertains to the experience of Mexican-descended individuals living in the US, but not all Mexican Americans identify as Chicano (The National Multicultural Institute).

Cisgender — A gender identity where an individual's self-perception of their gender aligns with their perceived sex (The National Multicultural Institute).

121

civil rights — Personal rights guaranteed and protected by the Constitution, e.g., freedom of speech and press and freedom from discrimination (The National Multicultural Institute).

classism — Biased attitudes and beliefs that result in, and help to justify, unfair treatment of individuals or groups because of their socioeconomic grouping. Classism can also be expressed as public policies and institutional practices that prevent people from breaking out of poverty rather than ensuring equal economic, social and educational opportunity (The National Multicultural Institute).

collusion — When people act to perpetuate oppression or prevent others from working to eliminate oppression, e.g., able-bodied people who object to strategies for making buildings accessible because of the expense.

colonialism — Control by individuals or groups over the territory/behavior of other individuals or groups. Imperialism refers to the political or economic control, either formally or informally, and creating an empire (The National Multicultural Institute).

colorblind — Term used to describe personal, group and institutional policies or practices that do not consider race or ethnicity as a determining factor. The term "colorblind" deemphasizes or ignores race and ethnicity as a large part of one's identity (The National Multicultural Institute).

cross-cultural — Refers to cultures around the world. There is no universally agreed-upon distinction between diversity and inclusion and cross-cultural work, although "cross-cultural" sometimes refers only to country or regional cultures rather than a broader definition of culture (The National Multicultural Institute).

cultural assimilation — An individual, family or group gives up certain aspects of its culture to adapt to the dominant culture; a process of learning that leads to the ability to effectively respond to the challenges and opportunities posed by the presence of social cultural diversity in a defined social system; knowledge, awareness and interpersonal skills that allow individuals to increase their understanding, sensitivity, appreciation and responsiveness to cultural differences and the interactions resulting from them; acquiring cultural competency varies among different groups and involves ongoing relational process tending to inclusion and trust-building; a process of learning that leads to the ability to effectively respond to the challenges and opportunities posed by the presence of social cultural diversity in a defined social system (The National Multicultural Institute).

cultural competency — A set of interpersonal skills that allow individuals to increase their understanding, sensitivity, appreciation and responsiveness to cultural differences and the interactions resulting from them. Cultural competence refers to an ability to interact effectively with people of different cultures. Cultural competence comprises four components: (1) awareness of one's own cultural worldview, (2) attitude toward cultural differences, (3) knowledge of different cultural practices and worldviews and (4) cross-cultural skills. Developing cultural competence results in an ability to understand, communicate with and effectively interact with people across cultures. Cultural competence is a development knowledge, awareness and interpersonal skills that allow individuals to increase their understanding, sensitivity, appreciation and responsiveness to cultural differences and the interactions resulting from them. (UC Berkeley Initiative for Equity, Inclusion, and Diversity).

cultural pluralism — Recognition of the contribution of each group to a common civilization. It encourages the maintenance and development of different life styles, languages and convictions. It strives to create the conditions of harmony and respect within a culturally diverse society (Institute for Democratic Renewal and Project Change).

culture — A pattern of thinking, feeling and acting learned early in one's life; a set of values that create rituals, symbols, heroes and so on. Culture is learned, very often hard to articulate and derived from one's social environment. A social system of meaning and custom that is developed by a group of people to assure its adaptation and survival. These groups are distinguished by a set of unspoken rules that shape values, beliefs, habits, patterns of thinking, behaviors and styles of communication (Institute for Democratic Renewal and Project Change).

denial — The refusal to acknowledge the societal privileges that are granted or denied based on an individual's identity components. Those who are in a stage of denial tend to believe "People are people. We are alike regardless of the color of our skin." In this way, the existence of a hierarchical system of privileges based on ethnicity or race are ignored (Institute for Democratic Renewal and Project Change).

differential consequences — Outcomes that are applied to different groups exhibiting identical behaviors, yet one group's behavior is valued and the other is devalued (The National Multicultural Institute).

differential validation — Validation of tests at different score levels for different classes of people. This is not tantamount to lowering standards for one or more groups to favor them over others. Differential validation occurs only where lower test scores by one class do predict a level of job performance equivalent to that predicted by the higher scores of another class (The National Multicultural Institute).

disability — A physical, mental or cognitive impairment or condition that qualifies under federal and state disability nondiscrimination laws for special accommodations to ensure programmatic and physical access. A physical or mental impairment, the perception of a physical or mental impairment or a history of having had a physical or mental impairment that substantially limits one or more major life activities (The Department of Justice).

discrimination — Acting or behaving based on prejudices when dealing with others. Unfavorable or unfair treatment toward an individual or group based on their race, ethnicity, color, national origin or ancestry, religion, socioeconomic status, education, sex, marital status, parental status, veteran's status, political affiliation, language, age, gender, physical or mental abilities, sexual orientation or gender identity (Sierra Club Employment Policy, Employee Handbook).

diversity — The full range of human and/or organizational differences and similarities. This includes, in part, dimensions such as age, culture, education, ethnicity, geography, gender, job level, job function, language, marital status, national origin, political affiliation, race, religion, sexual orientation, job skills, thought process and years of service. Diversity is generally defined as acknowledging, understanding, accepting, valuing and celebrating differences among people with respect to age, class, ethnicity, gender, physical and mental ability, race, sexual orientation, spiritual practice and public-assistance status. Diversity is the psychological, physical and social differences that occur among all individuals, including but not limited to race, ethnicity, nationality, religion, socioeconomic status, education, marital status, language, age, gender, sexual orientation, mental or physical ability and learning styles. A diverse group, community or organization is one in which a variety of social and cultural characteristics exist (The National Multicultural Institute).

diversity climate — The degree to which an organization implements fair human resource policies and socially integrates underrepresented employees. Diversity climate is a function of individual-level factors involving the extent of prejudice and stereotyping in organizations, group-intergroup factors referring to the degree of conflict between various groups within an organization and organizational-level factors regarding such domains as organizational culture. Diversity climate is also the degree that underrepresented personnel are integrated into higher-level positions and within an organization's social networks and whether institutional bias prevails in an organization's human resource systems such as recruiting, hiring, training, developing, promoting and compensating employees (The National Multicultural Institute).

diversity communication — The process of providing information to employees and managers regarding diversity and inclusion strategy and progress. Activities include conveying information via employee newsletters, closed-circuit television, employee focus groups, town-hall meetings, organization websites and social media (The National Multicultural Institute).

diversity competency — A process of learning that leads to an ability to effectively respond to the challenges and opportunities posed by the presence of social-cultural diversity in a defined social system (The National Multicultural Institute).

diversity management — A strategically driven process whose emphasis is on building skills, making quality decisions that bring out the best in every employee and assessing organizational mixtures and tensions because of changing workforce and customer demographics (The National Multicultural Institute).

diversity management initiatives — Proactive and intentional actions to get the best from the mix of employees, customers, suppliers and other stakeholders to achieve organizational objectives. Actions often include efforts to improve human resource processes and enhance organizational culture, such as how the organization recruits, hires, trains, mentors, promotes, develops and integrates employees (The National Multicultural Institute).

diversity management training — Intentional actions to educate a culturally diverse workforce and to sensitize employees and managers to differences in the organization such as gender, race and generation to maximize the potential productivity of all employees. Numerous organizations with these goals in mind have developed training programs such as Managing Diversity, Valuing Differences and Leading Diverse Work Teams (The National Multicultural Institute).

diversity metrics — The process of quantitatively and qualitatively measuring the impact of the organization's diversity strategy (The National Multicultural Institute).

diversity practitioner or professional — Individual responsible for managing the diversity and inclusion initiatives, or the chief diversity officer in an organization. This person has expertise in diversity and inclusion but may or may not be a full-time diversity professional (The National Multicultural Institute).

127

dominant culture — The most powerful cultural grouping. For example, in most parts of the United States, the dominant culture is composed of white, English-speaking, middle- to upper-income Christians (The National Multicultural Institute).

duty to accommodate — The obligation of an employer, service provider or union to take steps to eliminate disadvantage to employees, prospective employees or clients resulting from a rule, practice or physical barrier that has or may have an adverse impact on individuals or groups protected under state or federal law (The National Multicultural Institute).

empowerment — When target group members refuse to accept the dominant ideology and take actions to redistribute social power more equitably.

environmental equity — Measures the amelioration of the myriad inequities and disproportionate impacts that groups in society have faced, especially in the realm of environmental protection and access to nature and the environmental goods that aren't equally shared (The National Multicultural Institute).

equal access — Absence of barriers to admittance, such as those motivated by cultural or racial discrimination, to the institutions of a society. This includes access to services, programs and employment. To facilitate equal access, an outreach program is often needed to inform people that the program is available (The National Multicultural Institute).

equal employment opportunity — The process of administering human resource activities to ensure equal access in all phases of the employment process. Employment decisions are based solely on the individual merit and fitness of applicants and employees related to specific jobs, without regard to race, color, religion, sex, age, national origin, handicap, marital status or criminal record. Title VII of the Civil Rights Act of 1964 prohibits discrimination in any aspect of employment based on an individual's race, color, religion, sex or national origin (The National Multicultural Institute).

Equal Employment Opportunity Commission (EEOC) — The federal government agency mandated to enforce Title VII of the Civil Rights Act of 1964, as amended. The commission has five members, each appointed to a five-year term by the president of the United States with the advice and consent of Congress. The federal Equal Employment Opportunity Commission has the power to bring suits, subpoena witnesses, issue guidelines that have the force of law, render decisions, provide legal assistance to complainants and so on about fair employment (The National Multicultural Institute).

equal pay — As required by the Equal Pay Act of 1963 for employers subject to the Fair Labor Standards Act, businesses must provide equal pay for men and women performing the same or substantially similar jobs in the same establishment. For example, in a department store, a female salesperson in the ladies' shoe department must receive pay equal to that of a male salesperson in the men's shoe department (The National Multicultural Institute).

equality — Evenly distributed access to resources and opportunity necessary for a safe and healthy life; uniform distribution of access to ensure fairness.

equity — Equity is the principle of fair treatment, access, opportunity and advancement for people, while at the same time striving to identify and eliminate barriers that have prevented the full participation of some groups. The principle of equity acknowledges that there are historically underserved and underrepresented populations and that fairness regarding these unbalanced conditions is needed to assist equality in the provision of effective opportunities to all groups. The guarantee of fair treatment, access, opportunity and advancement while at the same time striving to identify and eliminate barriers that have prevented the full participation of some groups. The principle of equity acknowledges that there are historically underserved and underrepresented populations and that fairness regarding these unbalanced conditions is needed to assist equality in the provision of effective opportunities to all groups (UC Berkeley Initiative for Equity, Inclusion, and Diversity).

ESL — (E)nglish as a (S)econd (L)anguage; a term used to describe language learning programs in the United States for individuals for whom English is not their first or native language (The National Multicultural Institute).

essentialism — The practice of categorizing an entire group based on assumptions about what constitutes the "essence" of that group. Essentialism prevents individuals from remaining open to individual differences within groups (The National Multicultural Institute).

ethnic — An adjective used to describe groups that share a common language, race, customs, lifestyle, social view or religion. Everyone belongs to an ethnic group. The term is often confused with nonwhite. "Ethnic," however, refers to those traits that originate from racial, linguistic and cultural ties with a specific group (The National Multicultural Institute).

ethnicity — A social construct that divides people into smaller social groups based on characteristics such as values, behavioral patterns, language, political and economic interests, history and ancestral geographical base.

ethnocentrism — Characterized by, or based on, the attitude that one's own group is superior. Ethnocentric habitual disposition is to judge foreign peoples or groups by the standards or practices of one's own culture or ethnic group. The practice of using an ethnic group as a frame of reference, basis of judgment or standard criteria from which to view the world. Ethnocentrism favors one ethnic group's cultural norms and excludes the realities and experiences of other ethnic groups (The National Multicultural Institute).

eurocentrism — Reflecting a tendency to interpret the world in terms of Western, and especially European, values and experiences. The practice of using Europe and European culture as a frame of reference or standard criteria from which to view the world. Eurocentrism favors European cultural norms and excludes the realities and experiences of other cultural groups (The National Multicultural Institute).

feminism — Theory and practice that advocates for educational and occupational equity between men and women; undermines traditional cultural practices that support the subjugation of women by men and the devaluation of women's contributions to society (The National Multicultural Institute).

gay — People of the same sex who are attracted sexually and emotionally to each other. More commonly utilized to describe male attraction to other males. (The National Multicultural Institute)

gender — The socially constructed ideas about behavior, actions and roles a sex performs. Gender is a socially constructed system of classification that ascribes qualities of masculinity and femininity to people (The National Multicultural Institute).

gender characteristics — Gender characteristics can change over time and are different between cultures. Words that refer to gender include "man," "woman," "transgender," "masculine," "feminine" and "genderqueer." Gender also refers to one's sense of self as masculine or feminine, regardless of external genitalia. Gender is often conflated with sex; however, this is inaccurate, because "sex" refers to bodies, and "gender" refers to personality characteristics (The National Multicultural Institute).

gender identity — A personal conception of one's own gender; often in relation to a gender opposition between masculinity and femininity. Gender expression is how people externally communicate or perform their gender identity to others (The National Multicultural Institute).

global environmental racism — Race is a potent factor in sorting people into their physical environment and explaining social inequality, political exploitation, social isolation and quality of life. Racism influences land use, industrial facility siting, housing patterns, infrastructure development and who gets what, when, where and how much. Environmental racism refers to any policy, practice or directive that differentially affects or disadvantages (whether intended or unintended) individuals, groups or communities based on race or color (Second National People of Color Environmental Leadership Summit).

harassment — Unwelcome, intimidating, exclusionary, threatening or hostile behavior against an individual that is based on a category protected by law.

hazing — Verbal and physical testing, often of newcomers into a society or group, that may range from practical joking to tests of physical and mental endurance (The National Multicultural Institute).

heterosexism — Social structures and practices which serve to elevate and enforce heterosexuality while subordinating or suppressing other forms of sexuality.

Hispanic — A person, regardless of race, who is of Spanish culture or origin. This includes persons from Mexico, Central or South America, Puerto Rico, the Dominican Republic and Cuba. The US Census Bureau defines Hispanic as people who classify themselves in Spanish, Hispanic or Latino categories, which also include the subgroups Mexican, Mexican American, Chicano, Puerto Rican and Cuban (The National Multicultural Institute).

homophobia — The hatred or fear of homosexuals. It is characterized by negative attitudes and behaviors toward gays and lesbians and is expressed in a variety of ways, from insulting remarks and humor that reinforce stereotypes, to discrimination and violent behavior. A fear of individuals who are not heterosexual. Often results in hostile, offensive or discriminatory action against a person because they are gay, lesbian, bisexual, transgendered, queer identified or because they are perceived to be. These actions may be verbal or physical and can include insulting or degrading comments, taunts or "jokes" and excluding or refusing to cooperate with others because of their sexuality (The National Multicultural Institute).

human rights — Freedoms that are enjoyed by all people, simply because they are human. Human rights are supposed to apply equally to all people regardless of characteristics such as age, race or gender. The Universal Declaration of Human Rights extends these rights to all people around the world. The basic rights and freedoms to which all humans are entitled, often held to include the right to life and liberty, freedom of thought and expression, and equality before the law (The American Heritage Dictionary of the English Language).

identity group — A group, culture or community with which an individual identifies or shares a sense of belonging. Individual agency is crucial for identity development; no person should be pressured to identify with any existing group but instead have the freedom to self-identify on their own terms (The National Multicultural Institute).

inclusion — The act of creating environments in which any individual or group can be and feel welcomed, respected, supported and valued to fully participate. An inclusive and welcoming climate embraces differences and offers respect in words and actions for all people. Inclusion integrates the fact of diversity and embeds it into the core mission and institutional functioning. It is the active, intentional and ongoing engagement with diversity — in people, in the curriculum and in (intellectual, social, cultural and geographical) communities with which individuals might connect — in ways that increase one's awareness, content knowledge, cognitive sophistication and empathic understanding of the complex ways individuals interact within systems and institutions. The act of creating environments in which any individual or group can be and feel welcomed, respected, supported and valued to fully participate. An inclusive and welcoming climate embraces differences and offers respect in words and actions for all people (UC Berkeley Initiative for Equity, Inclusion, and Diversity).

inclusive language — Words of phrases that include all potential audiences from any identity group. Inclusive language does not assume or connote the absence of any group. An example of gender inclusive language is using "police officers" instead of "policemen" (The National Multicultural Institute).

inclusive leadership — The ability of managers (regardless of their human dimension of diversity) to get all the human and organizational mixes of an organization working better together for higher business and human outcomes.

indigenous — Originating from a culture with ancient ties to the land in which a group resides.

individual racism — Learned behavior taught through socialization, manifested in attitudes, beliefs and behaviors. The beliefs, attitudes and actions of individuals that support or perpetuate racism; can occur at both a conscious and unconscious level and can be active or passive. Examples include telling a racist joke, using a racial epithet or believing in the inherent superiority of whites.

institutional racism — Conscious or unconscious exercise of notions of racial superiority by social institutions through policies, practices, procedures, organizational culture and organizational values. Refers specifically to the ways in which institutional policies and practices create different outcomes for different racial groups. The institutional policies may never mention any racial group, but their effect is to create advantages for whites and oppression and disadvantage for people from groups classified as people of color.

An example includes city sanitation department policies that concentrate trash transfer stations and other environmental hazards disproportionately in communities of color.

intent vs. impact — This distinction is an integral part of inclusive environments; intent is what a person meant to do, and impact is the effect it had on someone else. Regardless of intent, it is imperative to recognize how behaviors, language, actions, etc. affect or influence other people. An examination of what was said or done and how it was received is the focus, not necessarily what was intended (Workforce Diversity Network).

internalized racism — Occurs in a racist system when a racial group oppressed by racism supports the supremacy and dominance of the dominating group by maintaining or participating in the set of attitudes, behaviors, social structures and ideologies that undergird the dominating group's power.

intersectionality — The ways in which oppressive institutions (racism, sexism, homophobia, transphobia, ableism, xenophobia, classism, etc.) are interconnected and cannot be examined separately from one another (African American Policy Forum).

"-isms" — A way of describing any attitude, action or institutional structure that subordinates

(oppresses) a person or group because of their target group: race (racism), gender (sexism), economic status (classism), age (ageism), religion, sexual orientation, language, etc.

Latino/a — Individual living in the United States originating from or having a heritage relating to Latin America (University of Maryland).

lesbian — A woman whose primary sexual attraction is to other women (UC Berkeley Gender Equity Resource Center).

LGBTQ (QIA) — Acronym for "Lesbian Gay Bisexual Transgender Queer (Questioning Intersex Allies)." The description of the movement expanded from gay and lesbian to LGBTQ and some include questioning, intersex, allies, same-gender-loving, asexual, pansexual and polyamorous.

marginalization — The placement of minority groups and cultures outside mainstream society. All that varies from the norm of the dominant culture is devalued and at times perceived as deviant and regressive (The National Multicultural Institute).

microaggression — The everyday verbal, nonverbal and environmental slights, snubs or insults, whether intentional or unintentional, that communicate hostile, derogatory or negative messages to target persons based solely upon their marginalized group membership.

multicultural — Of or pertaining to more than one culture (The National Multicultural Institute).

multiculturalism — Multiculturalism is an acknowledgment that, as people, we are culturally diverse and multifaceted, and a process through which the sharing and transforming of cultural experiences allows us to rearticulate and redefine new spaces, possibilities and positions for ourselves and others. There are many different — and sometimes conflicting — ideas around the highly contested term of "multiculturalism." While more mainstream discourses around diversity and multiculturalism have become abundant, such definitions — particularly when historical and asocial in their grounding — tend to miss parts of the picture and may thus unproductively disguise, and even reproduce (perhaps unintentionally), forms of injustice and oppression still prevalent in our society.

multicultural education — A long-term life commitment and dynamic process; it is for all people, it is inclusive, and it is the beginning of self-respect and respect of other cultures. It is building awareness, respect, interest and appreciation of the cultures of a variety of racial, ethnic and social groups and a willingness to create policies, programming and practices that encourage the expression, exchange of information and inclusion of differing cultural perspectives (The National Multicultural Institute).

neocolonization — Term for contemporary policies adopted by international and Western "First World" nations and organizations that exert regulation, power and control over "Third World" nations disguised as humanitarian help or aid. These policies are distinct but related to the "original" period of colonization of Africa, Asia and the Americas by European nations.

nonwhite — A protected group or protected classes that have been historically underrepresented in organizations or who have been oppressed or ignored in society, whether legislation exists to protect these groups. For equal-employment opportunity official reporting purposes, and for purposes of the workforce analysis required in Revised Executive Order No. 4, the term "nonwhite" includes blacks, Hispanics, Alaska Natives or American Indians and Asian or Pacific Islanders (The National Multicultural Institute).

nonwhite recruitment — Special recruitment efforts undertaken to assure that qualified protected class members are well represented in the applicant pools for positions from or in which they have been excluded or substantially underutilized. Such efforts may include contacting organizations and media with known protected-class constituencies. Open job posting and advertising and equal-opportunity employer statements necessary in many situations are matters of nondiscrimination rather than measures of affirmative action recruitment (The National Multicultural Institute).

norm — An ideal standard binding upon the members of a group and serving to guide, control or regulate power and acceptable behavior (Effective Philanthropy).

oppression — The systemic and pervasive nature of social inequality woven throughout social institutions as well as embedded within individual consciousness. Oppression signifies a hierarchical relationship in which dominant or privilege groups benefit, often in unconscious ways, from the disempowerment of subordinated or targeted groups (Adams, Bell and Griffin).

organizational climate — A measure (real or perceived) of the organization's work environment as it relates to interpersonal professional interactions. Climate refers to the experience of individuals and groups in an organization and the quality and extent of the interaction between those various groups and individuals. Diversity and inclusion efforts are not complete unless they also address climate. In a healthy climate, individuals and groups generally feel welcomed, respected and valued by the organization. A healthy climate is grounded in respect for others, nurtured by dialogue between those of differing perspectives and is evidenced by a pattern of civil interactions among community members. Not all aspects of a healthy climate necessarily feel positive — indeed, uncomfortable or challenging situations can lead to increased awareness, understanding and appreciation. Tension, while not always positive, can be healthy when handled appropriately. Conversely, in an unhealthy climate, individuals or groups often feel isolated, marginalized and even unsafe (The National Multicultural Institute).

organizational culture — A set of values within an organization that become practices. The rules of "how things get done here" can be both spoken and unspoken. The values of an organization are often based on the values of the company founders (The National Multicultural Institute).

organizational preference or tradition — Refers to the thinking or practices that are sometimes confused with requirements. An example of an organizational preference is a company almost always hiring employees with degrees from certain schools or universities, even though other schools offer comparable degrees (The National Multicultural Institute).

overt racism — Racism that is frank and open, including graffiti, intimidation or physical violence, and that legitimates negative racial stereotypes. Racial and ethnic slurs or so-called jokes are other examples of obvious racial discrimination. People often ignore racism because they do not know how to deal with it (The National Multicultural Institute).

Pan-Africanism — Describes the theory relating to the desire to educate all peoples of the African diaspora of their common plight and the connections between them. Some theorists promote linking all African countries across the continent through a common government, language, ideology or belief (University of Maryland).

pansexuality — A term reflective of those who feel they are sexually, emotionally and spiritually capable of falling in love with all genders (Queers United Activists).

people of color — A term defined by race or color only, not citizenship, place of birth, religion, language or cultural background. The term applies to people who are black, aboriginal, Chinese, South Asian, Southeast Asian, Filipino and Latin American Canadian and others. These terms are generally regarded as positive identities as opposed to "nonwhites," "minorities," "visible minorities" or "ethnics." Also known as "racially visible people" (The National Multicultural Institute).

person of color — Is not a term that refers to real biological or scientific distinction between people, but the common experience of being targeted and oppressed by racism. While each oppressed group is affected by racism differently and each group maintains its own unique identity and culture, there is also the recognition that racism has the potential to unite oppressed people in a collective of resistance. For this reason, many individuals who identify as members of racially oppressed groups also claim the political identity of being people of color. This in no way diminishes their specific cultural or racial identity; rather, it is an affirmation of the multiple layers of identity of every individual. This term also refrains from the subordinate connotation of triggering labels like "nonwhite" and "minority" (Office of Racial and Ethnic Concerns of Unitarian Universalist Association).

person with a disability — A person who has a physical or mental impairment that substantially limits one or more of such person's major life activities, has a record of such impairment or is regarded as having such an impairment. Also called "physically challenged person." See "physically challenged person" for further definitions as to the meaning of disability (The National Multicultural Institute).

physically challenged person — A person who has a physical or mental impairment that substantially limits one or more of such person's major life activities, has a record of such impairment or is regarded as having such an impairment. Also known as "person with a disability" (The National Multicultural Institute).

The following are general definitions as to the meaning of disability: "physical or mental impairment" means: (1) any physiological disorder or condition, cosmetic disfigurement or anatomical loss affecting one or more of the following body systems: neurological, musculoskeletal, special sense organs, respiratory (including speech organs), cardiovascular, reproductive, digestive, genitourinary, hemic and lymphatic, skin and endocrine; or (2) any mental or psychological disorder such as mental retardation, organic brain syndrome, emotional or mental illness and specific learning disabilities. The term "physical or mental impairment" includes, but is not limited to, such diseases and conditions as orthopedic, visual, speech and hearing impairments, cerebral palsy, epilepsy, muscular dystrophy, multiple sclerosis, cancer, heart disease, diabetes, mental retardation, emotional illness, drug addiction and alcoholism.

"Major life activities" means functions such as caring for oneself, performing manual tasks, walking, seeing, hearing, speaking, breathing, learning and working.

"Has a record of such impairment" means has a history of a mental or physical impairment that substantially limits one or more life activities.

"Is regarded as having an impairment" means: (1) has a physical or mental impairment that does not substantially limit major life activities but that is treated by an agency as constituting such a limitation;

142

(2) has a physical or mental impairment that substantially limits major life activities only because of the attitudes of others toward such impairment; or (3) has none of the impairments defined above but is treated by an agency as having such an impairment.

"Substantially limits" refers to the degree to which the impairment affects employability. A handicapped individual who is likely to have trouble in securing, retaining or advancing in employment will be considered substantially limited.

pluralism — A state of society in which members of diverse ethnic, racial, religious or social groups maintain an autonomous participation in and development of their traditional culture or special interest within the confines of a common civilization (The National Multicultural Institute).

polyamory — the practice or acceptance of having more than one intimate relationship at a time with the consent of all involved (Queers United Activists).

power — Access to resources, position, status, wealth or personal strength of character that gives a person, a group or a system the ability to influence others. Power can be used to affect others positively or negatively (The National Multicultural Institute).

prejudice — Prejudging another person, place or thing that is not backed with facts to substantiate the attitude or feeling; to prejudge a person or group negatively, usually without adequate evidence or information to substantiate the position. Frequently, prejudices are not recognized as false or unsound assumptions. Through repetition, they come to be accepted as common-sense notions and, when backed up with power, result in acts of discrimination and oppression. A prejudgment or unjustifiable, and usually negative, attitude of one type of individual or groups toward another group and its members. Such negative attitudes are typically based on unsupported generalizations (or stereotypes) that deny the right of individual members of certain groups to be recognized and treated as individuals with individual characteristics (Institute for Democratic Renewal and Project Change).

privilege — A special advantage, immunity or benefit not enjoyed by all and possibly not recognized by an individual or class of individuals. Power and advantages benefiting a group derived from the historical oppression and exploitation of other groups (University of Maryland).

protected classes — Groups identified in Executive Order No. 6 (nonwhites, women, disabled persons and Vietnam-era veterans) that are specifically protected against employment discrimination (The National Multicultural Institute).

queer — Term used to refer to people or culture of the lesbian, gay, bisexual, transgender community. A term once perceived as derogatory is now embraced by some members of the LGBTQ community (The National Multicultural Institute).

quotas — In employment law, court-ordered or court-approved hiring and/or promoting of specified numbers or ratios of nonwhites or women in positions from which a court has found they have been excluded because of unlawful discrimination. Quotas are not the same as goals and timetables (The National Multicultural Institute).

race — A social category used to classify humankind according to common ancestry or descent and reliant upon differentiation by general physical characteristics such as color of skin and eyes, hair type, stature and facial features. A social construct that artificially divides people into distinct groups based on characteristics such as physical appearance, ancestral heritage, cultural affiliation, cultural history, ethnic classification and the political needs of a society at a given period (Adams, Bell and Griffin).

race relations — Interaction between diverse racial groups within one society.

racial/ethnic groups — The four racial/ethnic groups protected by federal equal-employment opportunity laws are blacks, Hispanics, Asians or Pacific Islanders and American Indians or Alaska Natives. Racial/ethnic groups are defined by the federal government as follows:

- **white** (not of Hispanic origin) — Persons having origins in any of the original peoples of Europe, North Africa or the Middle East.
- **black** (not of Hispanic origin) — Persons having origins in any of the black racial groups of Africa.
- **Hispanic** — Persons of Mexican, Puerto Rican, Cuban, Central or South American or other Spanish culture or origin, regardless of race.
- **Asian or Pacific Islander**: Persons having origins in any of the original peoples of the Far East, Southeast Asia, the Indian Subcontinent, or the Pacific Islands. This area includes, for example, China, Japan, Korea, the Philippine Islands, and Samoa.
- **American Indian or Alaska Native** — Persons having origins in any of the original peoples of North America and who maintain cultural identification through tribal affiliation or community recognition.

racial equity — The condition that would be achieved if one's racial identity no longer influenced how one fares. Racial equity is one part of racial justice and must be addressed at the root causes and not just the manifestations. This includes the elimination of policies, practices, attitudes and cultural messages that reinforce differential outcomes by race or fail to eliminate them (Center for Assessment and Policy Development).

racial and ethnic identity — An individual's awareness and experience of being a member of a racial and ethnic group; the racial and the ethnic categories that an individual chooses to describe himself or herself based on such factors as biological heritage, physical appearance, cultural affiliation, early socialization and personal experience (Adams, Bell and Griffin).

racially visible people — A term defined by race or color only, not citizenship, place of birth, religion, language or cultural background. The term applies to people who are black, aboriginal, Chinese, South Asian, Southeast Asian, Filipino and Latin American Canadian and others. These terms are generally regarded as positive identities as opposed to "nonwhites," "minorities," "visible minorities" or "ethnics." Also known as "people of color" (The National Multicultural Institute).

racism — Individual and institutional practices and policies based on the belief that a race is superior to others. This often results in depriving certain individuals and groups of civil liberties, rights and other resources, hindering opportunities for social, educational and political advancement (The National Multicultural Institute).

racist society — A system of advantage based on race. A system of oppression based on race. A way of organizing society based on dominance and subordination based on race. Penetrates every aspect of personal, cultural and institutional life. Includes prejudice against people of color, as well as exclusion, discrimination against, suspicion of and fear and hate of people of color. Racism = Prejudice + the POWER to implement that prejudice (Exchange Project of the Peace & Development Fund).

representation — The results of intentional efforts to achieve a balanced workforce. It refers to an area of emphasis in diversity and inclusion where the goal is to ensure that people are hired based on their qualifications, thereby making the various business units, departments, teams and functions equitable regarding the various dimensions of diversity and/or making those dimensions mirror the labor market or customer base (The National Multicultural Institute).

reverse discrimination — Unfair treatment of members of a dominant or majority group. (Society of Human Resources Management); according to the National Multicultural Institute, this term is often used by opponents of affirmative action who believe that these policies are causing members of traditionally dominant groups to be discriminated against. The Supreme Court considers it to be illegal to consider race and other demographic categories in hiring and other employment related decisions (The National Multicultural Institute).

safe space — A space in which an individual or group may remain free of blame, ridicule and persecution and are in no danger of coming to mental or physical harm (The National Multicultural Institute).

147

selective perception — A subconscious process of noticing a specific behavior by one group while not noticing or dismissing the same behavior on the part of another group (The National Multicultural Institute).

sex — System of classification based on biological and physical differences, such as primary and secondary sexual characteristics. Differentiated from gender, which is based on the social construction and expectations of the categories "men" and "women" (University of Maryland).

sexism — Stems from a set of implicit or explicit beliefs, erroneous assumptions and actions based upon an ideology of inherent superiority of one gender over another and is evident within organizational or institutional structures and programs, as well as within individual thought or behavior patterns. Sexism, like racism, is a discriminatory act backed by power. Sexism is any act or institutional practice backed by institutional power that subordinates people because of gender (The National Multicultural Institute).

sexual harassment — Interference, intimidation or other offensive behavior from one work associate to another and based in part on the gender of the workers involved. The intent is to exert power over another (The National Multicultural Institute).

sexual orientation — The deep-seated direction of one's sexual (erotic) attraction toward the same gender, opposite gender or other genders. It is on a continuum and not a set of absolute categories. The direction of one's sexual attraction toward the same gender, opposite gender, or other genders. It is on a continuum and not necessarily a set of absolute categories (UC Berkeley Initiative for Equity, Inclusion, and Diversity).

social class — The hierarchical order of a society based on such indicators of social rank as income, occupation, education, ownership of property, family, religion and political relationships (The National Multicultural Institute).

social justice — This refers to the concept of a society that gives individuals and groups fair treatment and an equitable share of the benefits of society. A vision of society in which the distribution of resources is equitable, and all members are physically and psychologically safe and secure. Social justice involves social actors who have a sense of their own agency as well as a sense of social responsibility toward and with others and the society (Adams, Bell and Griffin).

social power — Access to resources that enhance chances of getting what one needs or influencing others to lead a safe, productive and fulfilling life (Adams, Bell and Griffin).

stereotype — A positive or negative set of beliefs held by an individual about the characteristics of a certain group (The National Multicultural Institute).

stereotyping — An extension of prejudice by labeling others based solely on their membership in a group and then labeling others like them in one broad characteristic, as if they have the same characteristic; also, false generalizations of a group of people that result in an unconscious or conscious categorization of members of that group. Stereotypes may be based upon misconceptions about ethnic, linguistic, geographical, religious and physical or mental attributes, as well as race, age, marital status and gender. Stereotyping is the tendency to lump together members of a group and to think of them as types rather than as individuals. All members of the group are falsely assumed to be alike, with exceptions being ignored or their existence denied. It is to generalize when we have an unpleasant experience with an individual belonging to a group. The resulting feelings of aversion and hostility, which may or may not be justified, are sometimes irrationally generalized to include all members of that group (The National Multicultural Institute).

systemic discrimination — A general condition, practice or approach that applies equally to the majority, but negatively affects opportunities or results for specific groups of people (The National Multicultural Institute).

tolerance — Acceptance and open-mindedness to different practices, attitudes and cultures; does not necessarily mean agreement with the differences (University of Maryland).

transgender — An individual whose gender identity differs from the societal expectations of their physical sex. Transgender or "trans" does not imply any form of sexual orientation. Cisgender is a gender identity where an individual's self-perception of their gender matches their sex. For example, a cisgendered female is a female with a female identity (The National Multicultural Institute).

underrepresented — Refers to groups who have been denied access and/or suffered past institutional discrimination in the United States and, according to the census and other federal measuring tools, includes African Americans, Asian Americans, Hispanics or Chicanos/Latinos and Native Americans. This is revealed by an imbalance in the representation of different groups in common pursuits such as education, jobs, housing and so on, resulting in marginalization for some groups and individuals and not for others relative to the number of individuals who are members of the population involved. Other groups in the United States have been marginalized and are currently underrepresented. These groups may include, but are not limited to, other ethnicities; adult learners; veterans; people with disabilities; lesbian, gay, bisexual and transgender individuals; people from different religious groups; and people from different economic backgrounds (The National Multicultural Institute).

underserved — Underserved populations are ones that are disadvantaged in relation to other groups because of structural or societal obstacles and disparities (The National Multicultural Institute).

United States Commission on Civil Rights — An independent, bipartisan agency established by Congress in 1957 and directed to: (1) investigate complaints alleging that citizens are being deprived of their right to vote by reason of their race, color, religion, sex, age, handicap or national origin, or by reason of fraudulent practices; (2) study and collect information concerning legal developments constituting discrimination or a denial of equal protection of the laws under the Constitution because of race, color, religion, sex, age, handicap or national origin, or in the administration of justice; (3) appraise federal laws and policies with respect to discrimination or denial of equal protection of the laws because of race, color, religion, sex, age, handicap or national origin, or in the administration of justice; (4) serve as a national clearinghouse for information in respect to discrimination or denial of equal protection of the laws because of race, color, religion, sex, age, handicap or national origin; and (5) submit reports, findings and recommendations to the president and Congress (The National Multicultural Institute).

151

values — General guiding principles that are to govern all activities; the way people should behave and the principles that should govern behavior.

valuing diversity — The recognition that it is not only ethical and fair to make one's organization accessible to all people but that their differences in identity, perspective, background and style are, in fact, valuable qualities and human resources that can significantly enrich and strengthen the organization and its capacity to achieve excellence (The National Multicultural Institute).

visually impaired — A phrase used to describe people who can only see very little. They see better with the assistance of technical aids such as magnifiers, telescopes, special glasses, and computers with special features such as large print (The National Multicultural Institute).

white fragility — Discomfort and defensiveness on the part of a white person when confronted by information on racial inequality and injustice (The National Multicultural Institute).

white privilege — refers to the unquestioned and unearned set of advantages, entitlements, benefits and choices bestowed on people solely because they are white. White people who experience such privilege may or may not be conscious of it (The National Multicultural Institute).

workforce diversity — Refers to ways in which people in a workforce are like and different from one another. In addition to the characteristics protected by law, other similarities and differences commonly cited include background, education, language skills, personality, sexual orientation and work role (The National Multicultural Institute).

workforce profile — An organizational snapshot illustrating the dispersion of race, national origin, gender and/or disability groups within specified employment categories.

xenophobia — Xenophobia is hatred, resistance and negative prejudice against foreign people and everything that is foreign (The National Multicultural Institute).

Appendix C — References

Acker, J. (2000). Gendered contradictions in organizational equity projects, *Organization*, vol. 7, no. 4, pp. 625–32.

Adams, M., Lee A. B., and Griffin, P. (Eds.) (1997). *Teaching for diversity and social justice: A sourcebook.* New York: Routledge. African American Policy Forum. "A primer on intersectionality." Available at http://www.whiteprivilegeconference.com/pdf/intersectionality_primer.pdf

Allard, M. J. (2002). Theoretical underpinnings of diversity. In C. Harvey and M. J. Allard (Eds.), *Understanding and managing diversity.* New Jersey: Prentice-Hall, pp. 3–27.

American Heritage Dictionary of English Language. Available at http://www.ahdictionary.com/

Ashkanasy, N. M., Hartel, C. E. J., and Daus, C. S. (2002). Diversity and emotion: The new frontiers in organizational behavior research, *Journal of Management*, vol. 28, no. 3, pp. 307–38.

Arredondo, P. (1996). *Successful diversity management initiatives: A blueprint for planning and implementation.* Thousand Oaks, CA: Sage.

Auyero, J. (2002). The judge, the cop, and the queen of carnival: Ethnography, storytelling, and the (contested) meanings of protest, *Theory and Society*, vol. 31, pp. 151–87.

Bacharach, S. B., Bamberger, P. A., and Vashdi, D. (2005). Diversity and homophily at work: supportive relations among white and African American peers, *Academy of Management Journal*, vol. 48, pp. 619–44.

Barmes, L., and Ashtiany, S. (2003). The diversity approach to achieving equality: Potential and pitfalls, *The Industrial Law Journal*, vol. 32, pp. 274–96.

Basu, S. J., and Barton, A. C. (2007). Developing a sustained interest in science among urban minority youth, *Journal of Research in Science Teaching*, vol. 44, no. 3, pp. 466–89.

Baytos, L. M. (1995). *Designing & Implementing Successful Diversity Programs*. Englewood Cliffs, NJ: Prentice Hall.

Bivens, D. (1995). Internalized racism: A definition. Women's Theological Center. Available at http://www.thewtc.org/publications.html

Bell, E. L. J., and Nkomo, S. M. (2001). *Our separate ways: Black and white women and the struggle for professional identity*. Boston, MA: Harvard Business School Press.

Bhuiyan, J. (28 March 2017). Uber has published its much sought-after diversity numbers for the first time. *Recode*.

Blackmon, D. A. (2008). *Slavery by another name*. New York: Anchor Books.

Brief, A. (2000). Establishing a climate for diversity: the inhibition of prejudiced reactions in the workplace. In G. Ferris, *Research in personnel and human resource management*, vol. 19, pp. 91–129.

155

Brittain, J. L. (2002). *Managerial effectiveness in a global context.* Greensboro, NC: Center for Creative Leadership.

Bronson, P., and Merryman, A. (5 September 2009). Even babies discriminate: A Natureshock excerpt, *Newsweek* Available at https://www.newsweek.com/even-babies-discriminate-nur-tureshock-excerpt-79233

Brown, V. R., Shriberg, A., and Lloyd, C. (1998). *Diversity councils that work: A workbook for success.* Cincinnati, OH: Global Lead Management Consulting.

Bucher, R., & Bucher, P. (2003). *Diversity consciousness: Opening our minds to people, cultures, and opportunities.* New York: Prentice Hall.

Bureau of Justice Statistics. (n.d.) Arrest-Related Deaths. Retrieved May 17, 2016, from: http://www.bjs.gov/index.cfm?ty=dcdetail &iid=428

Campbell, B. (2003). *Beyond 9/11 Christians & Muslims together.* Atlanta: The Community Institute Press.

Carnevale, A. P., and Stone, S.C. (1995). *American mosaic: An in-depth report on the future of diversity at work.* New York: McGraw-Hill.

Carr-Ruffino, N. (1996) *Managing diversity: Skill builder.* Cincinnati, OH: Thomson Executive Press, (ITP).

Carr-Ruffino, N. (2002). *Managing diversity: People skills for a multicultural workplace* (5th ed.). Needham Heights, MA: Pearson Custom.

Carter, R. T. (Ed.) (2000). *Addressing cultural issues in organizations: Beyond the corporate context.* Thousand Oaks, CA: Sage.

Census Bureau. (2012, April 25). 2010 census shows interracial and interethnic married couples grew by 28 percent over decade. Retrieved May 17, 2016 from: https://www.census.gov/newsroom/releases/archives/2010_census/cb12-68.html

Center for Anti-Oppressive Education. Definition of anti-oppressive education. Available at http://antioppressiveeducation.org/definition.html

Center for Assessment and Policy Development. Evaluation tools for racial equality terms and vocabulary. Available at http://www.evaluationtoolsforracialequity.org/termRacial.htm

Cianciotto, J. (23 December 2015). When discrimination costs $400 billion annually. *The Huffington Post.*

Clair, J. A., Beatty, J. E., and Maclean, T. L. (2005). Out of sight but not out of mind: managing invisible social identities in the workplace, *Academy of Management Review*, vol. 30, pp. 78–95.

Clutterbuck, D., and Ragins, B. R. (2002). *Mentoring and diversity: An international perspective.* Woburn, MA: Butterworth-Heinemann.

Cohen, C. J. (1999). *The boundaries of blackness: AIDS and the breakdown of black politics.* Chicago: University of Chicago Press.

Connor, M. (8 February 2017). Tech still doesn't get diversity: Here's how to fix it. *Wired.*

Cox, T. (1993). *Cultural diversity in organizations: Theory, research & practice.* San Francisco: Berrett-Koehler.

Cox, T., Jr., and Beale, R. L. (1997). *Developing competency to manage diversity.* San Francisco: BerrettKoehler.

Crenshaw, K. (1991). Mapping the margins: intersectionality, identity politics, and violence against women of color, *Stanford Law Review*, vol. 43, no. 6, pp. 1241–99.

Crime Statistics. (n.d.). Retrieved May 17, 2016 from: https://www.fbi.gov/stats-services/crimestats

Cross, E. Y. (2000). *Managing diversity: The courage to lead.* Westport, CT: Quorum Books (Greenwood).

Cross, E. Y., and White, M. B. (Eds.) (2008). The diversity factor: Capturing the competitive advantage of a changing workforce. Chicago: Irwin, 1996. Department of Justice. "Americans with Disabilities Act of 1990, As Amended." Available at http://www.ada.gov/pubs/ada.htm

Dalton, M. (2002). *Success for the new global manager: What you need to know to work across distances, countries, and cultures.* San Francisco: Jossey-Bass.

DeAngelis, T. (2009). Unmasking racial micro-aggressions. *Monitor on Psychology*, vol. 40, no. 2, p. 42.

Department of Justice. (1974). Report of the national advisory commission on civil disorders. Retrieved from https://www.ncjrs.gov/pdffiles1/Digitization/8073NCJRS.pdf

Department of Justice. (2015, March 4). Department of justice report regarding the criminal investigation into the shooting death of Michael Brown by Ferguson, Missouri police officer Darren Wilson. Retrieved from https://www.justice.gov/sites/default/files/opa/press-releases/attachments/2015/03/04/doj_report_on_shooting_of_michael_brown_1.pdf

Dismantling Racism Institute. *A resource book for social change groups.* Western States Center, 2003. Available at http://www.postoilsolutions.org/documents/dismantling_racism_resource-book_western_states_center.pdf

Douglas, C. A. (2003). *Key events and lessons for managers in a diverse workforce: A report on research and findings.* Greensboro, NC: Center for Creative Leadership,

Effective Philanthropy. Naming norm. Available at http://www.effectivephilanthropybook.org/concepts/namingnorm.html

Englemeier, S. (2012). *Inclusion: The new competitive business advantage.* Minneapolis, MN: Inclusion NC Media.

Espinal, I. (2001). A new vocabulary for inclusive librarianship: applying whiteness theory to our profession. In L. Castillo-Speed (Ed.), *The power of language/El poder de la palabra: selected papers from the Second REFORMA National Conference* (pp. 131–49). Englewood, CO: Libraries Unlimited.

Eveline, J., & Todd, P. (2002). Teaching managing diversity via feminist theory, *International Journal of Inclusive Education*, vol. 6, pp. 33–46.

Fenn, J., and Irvin, C. J. (2005). *Do you see what I see? A diversity tale for retaining people of color.* San Francisco: John Wiley & Sons.

Ferdman, B. M. (Ed.), and Deane, B. R. (Assoc. Ed.) (2013). *Diversity at work: The practice of inclusion.* San Francisco: Jossey-Bass.

Fisher v. University of Texas at Austin et al., 570 U. S. 320 (2013).

Frasse-Blunt, M. (2003). Thwarting the diversity backlash: Develop an inclusive plan that highlights the bottom-line effect and benefits to all employees, *HR Magazine*, vol. 48, no. 6, pp. 37–42.

Frickel, S. (2011). Who are the experts of environmental health justice? In G. Ottinger and B. R. Cohen (Eds.), *Technoscience and environmental justice: Expert cultures in a grassroots movement* (pp. 21–40). Cambridge, MA: MIT Press.

Frost, S. (2014). *The inclusion imperative: How real inclusion creates better business and builds better societies.* Philadelphia, PA: Kogan Page Ltd.

Galvan, A. (2015). Soliciting performance, hiding bias: Whiteness and librarianship. In the Library with the Lead Pipe. Retrieved from http://www.inthelibrarywiththeleadpipe.org/2015/soliciting-performance-hiding-bias-whiteness-and-librarianship/

Gardenswartz, L., and Rowe, A. (1993). *Managing diversity: A complete desk reference and planning guide.* Homewood, IL: Business One Irwin and San Diego Pfeiffer.

Gardenswartz, L., and Rowe, A. (1994). *Diverse teams at work: Capitalizing on the power of diversity.* Chicago: Irwin.

Gardenswartz, L., et al. (2003). *The global diversity desk reference: Managing an international workforce.* San Francisco: Jossey-Bass, 2003.

Garibay, J. C. (2014). Diversity in the classroom. Los Angeles, CA: UCLA Diversity & Faculty Development. Retrieved from https://faculty.diversity.ucla.edu/resources-for/teaching/diversity-in-the-classroom-booklet

Gentile, M. C. (Ed.) (1994). *Differences that work: Organizational excellence through diversity.* Boston: Harvard Business School Publishing.

Gilmore, R. W. (2007). In the shadow of the shadow state. In *Incite! Women of color against violence, the revolution will not be funded: Beyond the non-profit industrial complex* (pp. 41–52). Cambridge, MA: South End Press.

Goode, S. J., and Baldwin, J. N. (2005). Predictors of African American representation in municipal government, *Review of Public Personnel Administration*, vol. 25, no. 1, pp. 29–55.

Goode, S. J. (2011). *So, you think you can teach: A guide for new college professors on how to teach adult learners.* Bloomington: iUniverse Books.

Goode, S. J. (2014). *Diversity managers: Angels of mercy or barbarians at the gate.* Bloomington: iUniverse Books.

Hacker. A. (2003). *Two nations: Black & white, separate, hostile, unequal.* New York: Scribner

Hansen, F. (2003). Diversity's business case doesn't add up, *Workforce*, pp. 28–32.

Hayles, V. R., and Russell, A. M. (1997). *Diversity directive: Why some initiatives fail and what to do about it.* Chicago: Irwin.

Henderson, G. (1994). *Cultural diversity in the workplace.* Westport, CT: Quorum Books.

Herman, R. E. (1999). *Keeping good people: Strategies for solving the #1 problem facing business today.* Winchester, VA: Oakhill Press.

Hill, D. (2010). Class, capital and education in this neoliberal and neoconservative period. In S. Macrine, P. Maclaren, and D. Hill (Eds.), *Revolutionizing pedagogy: Education for social justice within and beyond global neo-liberalism* (pp. 119–144). New York: Palgrave Macmillan.

Honma, T. (2005). Trippin' over the color line: The invisibility of race in library and information studies, *InterActions: UCLA Journal of Education and Information Studies*, vol. 1, no. 2, pp. 1–26. Retrieved from https://escholarship.org/uc/item/4nj0w1mp.pdf

Howarth, C. (1999). *Monitoring poverty and social exclusion.* York, PA: Joseph Rowntree Foundation.

Horvath, R. J. (February 1972). A definition of colonialism, *Current Anthropology*, vol. 13, no. 1. Available at http://www.clas.ufl.edu/users/marilynm/Theorizing_Black_America_Syllabus_files/Definition_of_Colonia lism.pdf

Hubbard, E. E. (2004). *The diversity scorecard: Evaluating the impact of diversity on organizational performance.* Burlington, MA: Elsevier Butterworth-Heinemann.

Institute for Corporate Diversity. (1996). *Diversity in corporate America: The comprehensive desk reference.* Minneapolis, MN: Institute for Corporate Diversity.

Institute for Democratic Renewal and Project Change Anti-Racism Initiative. (2001). A community builder's tool kit: 15 tools for creating healthy, productive interracial/multicultural communities. Claremont, CA: Claremont Graduate University, pp. 32–33. Available at http://www.capd.org/pubfiles/pub2004-07-03.pdf

Institutional racism. (2014). In J. Scott (Ed.), *A dictionary of sociology.* Retrieved from http://0-www.oxfordreference.com/view/10.1093/acref/9780199683581.001.0001/acref-9780199683581-e-1125

Jackson, S. E. (1992). *Diversity in the workplace: Human resources initiatives.* New York: Guilford.

Jacobs, B. A. (2007). *Race manners for the 21st century: Navigating the minefield between black and white Americans in an age of fear* (2nd Ed.). New York: Arcade Publishing.

Jamieson, D., and O'Mara, J. (1991). *Managing workforce 2000: Gaining the diversity advantage.* San Francisco: Jossey-Bass.

Jayson, S. (26 April 2012). Census shows big jump in interracial couples. *USA Today.* Retrieved May 17, 2016, from: http://usatoday30.usatoday.com/news/nation/story/2012-04-24/census-interracial-couples/54531706/1

Josey, E. J. (1972). Libraries, reading, and the liberation of black people, *The Library Scene*, vol. 1, no. 1, pp. 4–7.

Kaplan, M., and Donovan, M. (2013). *Inclusion dividend: Why investing in diversity & inclusion pays off.* Brookline, MA: Bibliomotion, Inc.

Kendall, F. E. (2013). *Understanding white privilege: Creating pathways to authentic relationships across race.* New York: Routledge Taylor and Francis Group.

King, M. A., Sims, A., and Osher, D. How is cultural competence integrated in education? Available at http://cecp.air.org/cultural/Q_integrated.htm

Koulopoulos, T., and Keldsen, D. (2014). *The Gen Z effect: The six forces shaping the future of business.* Boston: Bibliomotion

Kranich, N. (2001). Equality and equity of access: What's the difference? American Library Association. Available at http://www.ala.org/offices/oif/iftoolkits/toolkitrelatedlinks/equalityequity

Kusku, F., Özbilgin, M. F., and Özkale, L. (2007). Against the tide: Gendered prejudice and disadvantage, in engineering study from a comparative perspective, *Gender, Work and Organization*, vol. 14, no. 2, pp. 109–29.

Lasch-Quinn, E. (2001). *Race experts: How racial etiquette, sensitivity training, and new age therapy hijacked the civil rights revolution.* New York: W. W. Norton & Company.

Lazzaro, A. E., Mills, S., Garrard, T., Ferguson, E., Watson, M., and Ellenwood, D. (2014). Cultural competency on campus: Applying

ACRL's Diversity Standards. *College and Research Libraries News*, vol. 75, no. 6, 332–35. Retrieved from http://crln.acrl. org/content/75/6/332.full

Leach, J., Bette, G., Jackson, T., and LaBella, A. (1995). *A practical guide to working with diversity: The process, the tools, the resources.* New York: AMACOM.

Lee, O., and Buxton, C. A. (2010). *Diversity and equity in science education: Research, policy, and practice.* New York: Teachers College Press.

Livers, A. B., and Caver, K. A. (2003). *Leading in black and white: Working across the racial divide in corporate America.* San Francisco: Jossey Bass

Llewellyn, N. (2001). The role of storytelling and narrative in a modernization initiative, *Local Government Studies*, vol. 27, no. 4, pp. 35–58.

Loden, M. (1996). *Implementing diversity.* Chicago: Irwin.

Loden, M., and Rosener, J. B. (1991). *Workforce America! Managing employee diversity as a vital resource.* Homewood, IL: Business One Irwin.

Lyon, G. H., Jafri, J., and St. Louis, K. (2012). *Beyond the pipeline: STEM pathways for youth development.* Afterschool Matters, vol. 16, pp. 48–57.

Manji, I. (2003). *The trouble with Islam today.* New York: St. Martin's Press.

McLellan, H. (2006). Corporate storytelling perspectives, *The Journal for Quality and Participation*, Spring, pp. 17–20.

McMahon, A. (2010). Does workplace diversity matter? A survey of empirical studies on diversity and firm performance 2000–2009, *Journal of Diversity Management*, vol. 5, no. 2, pp. 37–48.

Miller, F. A., and Katz, J. H. (2002) *The inclusion breakthrough.* San Francisco: Berrett Koehler Publishers.

Morrison, A. M. (1996). *The new leaders: Leadership diversity in America.* San Francisco: Jossey-Bass.

Morrison, A. M., and Crabtree, K. M. (1993). *Developing diversity in organizations: A digest of select literature.* Greensboro, NC: Center for Creative Leadership.

Morrison, A. M., Ruderman, M. N. and Hughes-James, M. (2003). Making diversity happen: Controversies and solutions. Greensboro, NC: Center for Creative Leadership, 1993. National Multicultural Institute. "Diversity Terms." Available at https://our.ptsem.edu/UploadedFiles/Multicultural/MCRDiversityTerms.pdf

Myers, J. (2000). *Afraid of the dark: What whites and blacks need to know about each other.* Chicago: Lawrence Hill Books.

Nadler, D. A., and Tushman, M. L. (1990). Beyond the charismatic leader: Leadership and organizational change, *California Management Review*, Winter, pp. 77–97.

National Urban League. *The state of black America 2007.* Springfield: Berkham Publications Group.

NBC News. (2017). Uber CEO caught on camera arguing with driver over prices. NBCNews.com.

Newcomer, E. Uber's loss exceeds $800 million in third quarter on $1.7 billion in net revenue. Bloomberg.com. Bloomberg, 19 Dec. 2016. Web. 11 Apr. 2017.

New York Times. (2000). How race is lived in America. Available at https://archive.nytimes.com/www.nytimes.com/library/national/race/

Obama, M., (9 June 2015). Remarks by the First Lady at Martin Luther King Jr. Preparatory High School Commencement Address. Speech presented at Martin Luther King Jr. Preparatory High School Commencement, Chicago, IL. Retrieved from https://www.whitehouse.gov/the-press-office/2015/06/09/remarks-first-lady-martin-luther-king-jr-preparatory-high-school- commence

Obergefell et al. v. Hodges, Director, Ohio Department of Health, et. al., 576 U. S. 228 (2015).

Ochs, R. "Bisexual resources." Available at http://www.robynochs.com/resources/Bisexual.html, Office of Racial and Ethnic Concerns of Unitarian Universalist Association. "Identity-based ministries." Unitarian Universalist Association, 2007. Available at http://www.uua.org/directory/staff/multiculturalgrowth/

Page, S. E. (2007). *The difference: How the power of diversity creates better groups, firms, schools, and societies.* Princeton, NJ: Princeton University Press.

Parkin, M. (2004). *Tales for change: Using storytelling to develop people and organizations.* London: Kogan Page.

Pho, A., and Masland, T. (2014). The revolution will not be stereo-typed: Changing perceptions through diversity. In N. Pagowsky and M. Rigby (Eds.), *The librarian stereotype: Deconstructing percep-tions & presentations of information work* (pp. 257–82). Chicago: Association of College and Research Libraries. Retrieved from http://pdxscholar.library.pdx.edu/cgi/viewcontent.cgi?arti-cle=1164&context=ulib_fac

Poole, P. J. (1997). *Diversity: A business advantage: A practical guide.* Ajax, Ontario: Poole.

Potapchuk, M., Leiderman, S., Bivens, D., and Major, B. (2005). Flipping the script: White privilege and community building, Center for Assessment and Policy Development. Available at http://www.capd.org/pubfiles/pub-2005-01-01.pdf

Prince, D. W., and Hoppe, M. H. (2008). Communicating across cultures. Greensboro, NC: Center for Creative Leadership, 2000. Queers United Activists. "Diversity 101." Available at http://queer-sunited.blogspot.com/2008/06/diversity-lesson-101-pansexual-ity.html

Ready, D. A. (2002). How storytelling builds next-generation lead-ers, *MIT Sloan Management Review*, Summer, pp. 63–69.

Richard, O. C., and Murthi, B. P. S. (2004). Does race matter within a multicultural context? Alternate modes of theorizing and theory testing, Academy of Management Best Conference Paper, GDO: C1–C6.

Richardson, V. (21 April 2015). Police kill more whites than blacks, but minority deaths generate more outrage, *Washington Times*. Retrieved from http://www.washingtontimes.com/news/2015/apr/21/police-kill-more-whites-than-blacks-but-minority-d/?page=all

Ridley, C., and Kelly, S. (2006). Institutional racism. In Y. Jackson (Ed.), *Encyclopedia of multicultural psychology* (pp. 256–58). Thousand Oaks, CA: SAGE Publications, Inc. doi: http://0-dx.doi.org.libraries.colorado.edu/10.4135/9781412952668.n131

Robbins, S. L. (2007). *Teachable moments: Short stories to spark diversity dialogue.* Otsego, MI: Page Free Publishing, Inc.

Rodriquez v. United States, 575 U.S. 473 (2015).

Rogers, J. O. (2015). *Epiphany.* North Charleston, North Carolina: Independent Publishing Platform.

Rosen, E. (2007). *The culture of collaboration: Maximizing time, talent and tools to create value in the global economy.* San Francisco: Red Ape Publishing.

Rosener, J. B. (1995). *America's competitive secret: Utilizing women as a management strategy.* New York: Oxford University Press.

Ross, H. J. (2011). *Reinventing diversity: Transforming organizational community to strengthen people, purpose, and performance.* Lanham, MD: Rowman & Littlefield Publishers, Inc.

Rothstein, R. (15 October 2014). The making of Ferguson, *The American Prospect*. Retrieved from http://prospect.org/article/making-ferguson-how-decades-hostile-policy-created-powder-kegmagazine

Ruderman, M. N., Hughes-James, M. W., and Jackson, A. E. (Eds.). (1996). *Selected research on work team diversity*. Washington, DC: American Psychological Association.

Sierra Club Employee Handbook. (2013). Available at http://club-house.sierraclub.org/administration/hr/handbooks-guides/

Simons, G. F., ázquez, C., and Harris, P. R. (1993). *Transcultural leadership: Empowering the diverse workforce*. Houston: Gulf.

Simons, G. F., Abramms, B., and Hopkins, L. A. (1996). *Cultural diversity fieldbook: Fresh visions and breakthrough strategies for revitalizing the workplace*. Princeton, NJ: Peterson's/Pacesetter Books.

Solorzano, D. G., and Yosso, T. J. (2002). Critical race methodology: Counter-storytelling as an analytical framework for education research, *Qualitative Inquiry*, vol. 8, no. 1, pp. 23–44.

Solorzano, D., and Huber, L. (2012). Microaggressions, racial. In J. Banks (Ed.), *Encyclopedia of diversity in education* (pp. 1489–92). Thousand Oaks, CA: SAGE Publications, Inc. Retrieved from http://0-knowledge.sagepub.com/view/diversityineducation/n472.xml

Sonnenschein, W. (1999). *The diversity toolkit: How you can build and benefit from a diverse workforce*. New York: McGraw-Hill.

References

South, O., and White, M. B. (Eds.). (1995). *The diversity factor reading book: Selections from the diversity factor.* Teaneck, NJ: The Diversity Factor.

Sowell, P. H. (2009). *None of us is as good as all of us: How McDonald's prospers by embracing inclusion and diversity.* San Francisco: Jossey-Bass.

Smedley, A., and Smedley, B. D. (2005). Race as biology is fiction, racism as a social problem is real: Anthropological and historical perspectives on the social construction of race, *American Psychologist*, vol. 60, no. 1, pp. 16–26.

Sue, D. W., Capodilupo, C. M., Torino, G. C., Bucceri, J. M., Holder, A. M. B., Nadal, K. L., and Esquilin, M. (2007). Racial microaggressions in everyday life: Implications for clinical practice, *American Psychologist*, vol. 62, no. 4, pp. 271–86.

Tannen, D. (1994). *Talking from 9 to 5.* New York: William Morrow.

Tatum, B. D. (1997). *Why are all the black kids sitting together in the cafeteria? A psychologist explains the development of racial identity.* New York: Basic Books.

Taylor, C. (2001). *Creating the multicultural organization: A strategy for capturing the power of diversity.* San Francisco: Jossey-Bass.

Taylor, C., and Beale, R. B. (1997). Developing competency to manage diversity: Readings cases and activities. San Francisco: Berrett-Koehler Publishers, and Emeryville, CA: Publishers Group West [distributor].

Thiederman, S. (1991). *Bridging cultural barriers for corporate success: How to manage the multicultural work force.* Lexington, KY: Lexington Books.

Thiederman, S. (1991). *Profiting in America's multicultural marketplace: How to do business across cultural lines.* New York: Macmillan.

Thiederman, S. B. (2003). *Making diversity work: 7 steps for defeating bias in the workplace.* Chicago: Dearborn. Available at http://www.learncom.com/pdf/VL6777.pdf

Thiederman, S. B. (2013). *The diversity and inclusion handbook.* Flower Mound, TX: The Walk the Talk Company.

Thomas, R. R. (1990). From affirmative action to affirming diversity, *Harvard Business Review*, vol. 68, no. 2, pp. 107–117.

Thomas Jr., R. R. (1991). *Beyond race and gender: Unleashing the power of your total workforce by managing diversity.* New York: Amacom.

Thomas Jr., R. R. (1996). Redefining diversity, *HR Focus*, April, pp. 6–7.

Thomas Jr., R. R. (1999). Diversity management, *Executive Excellence*, vol. 16, pp. 8–9.

Thomas, R. R., Jr. (2006). *Building on the promise of diversity: How we can move to the next level in our workplaces, our communities, and our society.* New York: AMACOM.

Thomas, R. R. (1992). *Differences do make a difference.* Atlanta: The American Institute for Managing Diversity.

Thomas, R. R. (1996). *Redefining diversity.* New York: American Management Association.

Thomas, R. R., and Woodruff, M. I. (1999). *Building a house for diversity: How a fable about a giraffe and elephant offers new strategies for today's workforce.* New York: AMACOM.

Trepagnier, B. (2006). *Silent racism.* Boulder, CO: Paradigm Publishers.

University of Maryland. "Diversity Dictionary." Moving Towards Community. (2001). Available at http://www.inform.umd.edu/ EdRes/Topic/Diversity/Reference/divdic.html.

Vance, C. M. (1991). Formalizing storytelling in organizations: A key agenda for the design of training, *Journal of Organizational Change Management*, vol. 4, no. 3, pp. 52–58.

Wang, W. (2012). The rise of intermarriage, rates, characteristics vary by race and gender. Retrieved May 17, 2016, from http://www.pewsocialtrends.org/2012/02/16/the-rise-of-intermarriage/

Watson, J. (2006). *Without excuses: Unleash the power of diversity to build your business.* New York: St. Martin's Press.

Wing, S. D. (2010). Racial microaggressions in everyday life. Available at https://www.psychologytoday.com/blog/microaggressions-in-everyday-life/201010/racialmicroaggressions-in-everyday-life

Wilson, T. (1996). *Diversity at work: The business case for equity.* New York: John Wiley & Sons.

Wise, T. (2008). *White like me: Reflections on race from a privileged son.* Berkeley: Soft Skull Press.

Wittmer, J. (Ed.). (2013). *Valuing diversity and similarity: Bridging the gap through interpersonal skills.* Minneapolis, MN: Educational Media, 1992. Workforce Diversity Network. "Professional Resources." Available at http://www.workforcediversitynetwork.com/res_articles.aspx

Zemke, R., Raines, C., and Filipczak, B. (2000). *Generations at work: Managing the clash of veterans, boomers, Xers, and nexters in your workplace.* New York: AMACOM American Management Association.

About the Author

Dr. Shelton Goode is a diversity leader with over twenty years of human resource and business experience. He has held executive HR positions for companies ranging in size from $300 million to $11 billion–plus and has developed or implemented talent-management programs, performance management systems, sales incentive plans, labor relations strategies and large-scale culture-change initiatives. As a result, he has earned a reputation as a strategic yet results-oriented HR and business leader.

Dr. Goode learned the value of diversity and inclusion firsthand by rolling up his sleeves and providing CEOs and senior executives with counsel, insight, resources, tools and innovative ideas that helped advance their companies' strategic business goals. For the last ten years, he has leveraged his seasoned leadership and consulting skills to help companies implement diversity and inclusion initiatives that enhanced their talent acquisition, employee retention and employee engagement strategies.

Dr. Goode has also used his knowledge and experience to teach and mentor others. In 1993, he was awarded the first-ever African-American Doctoral Fellowship by Troy University and began teaching at the university in 1996. Since that time, he has been dedicated to helping adult learners achieve their educational goals. For example, as an adjunct professor at Troy University, Dr. Goode taught thousands of students in the school's master's in public administration program. His teaching excellence was recognized when he received the school's prestigious Faculty Member of the Year Award in 2005. Dr. Goode leveraged his extensive teaching experience to publish his first book, *So, You Think You Can Teach: A Guide for the New College Professor in Teaching Adult Learners.* He is also

175

the founder and CEO of My ABD Network, an organization that helps students succeed in doctoral education programs.

Dr. Goode, a highly decorated Air Force veteran, has not only served the country in time of war but also consistently served his community in time of need. In July 2011, the Supreme Court of Georgia appointed him to the State Bar Ethics Investigative Panel. He was one of only three non-lawyers serving on this prestigious panel. He chaired the Conference Board Diversity and Inclusion Leadership Council and has served on the board of numerous professional organizations, such as the Atlanta Compliance and Ethics Roundtable, American Association of Blacks in Energy, Society for Human Resource Management and Atlanta and Diversity Management Advocacy Group. The National Association of African Americans in Human Resources awarded him their HR Trailblazer Award in 2005 and 2012 — he was the only person selected for the award twice. In April 2013, the Technology Association of Georgia presented him with the organization's first Lifetime Achievement Award for his body of work in diversity and inclusion and human resources.

Dr. Goode received his bachelor's degree from Southwest Texas State University (now Texas State University) and his master's degree in human resource management from Troy University. He obtained his doctorate in public administration from the University of Alabama. Dr. Goode speaks nationally on a variety of human resource management and diversity topics.

Index

CPSIA information can be obtained
at www.ICGtesting.com
Printed in the USA
FFHW022309151218
49898966-54500FF